$\mathscr{F}$RANTIC TRANSMISSIONS
TO AND FROM LOS ANGELES

Also by Kate Braverman

Frantic Transmissions

to and from

Los Angeles

· An Accidental Memoir ·

Kate Braverman (signature)

Graywolf Press

SAINT PAUL, MINNESOTA

Publication of this volume is made possible in part by a grant provided by the Minnesota State Arts Board, through an appropriation by the Minnesota State Legislature; a grant from the Wells Fargo Foundation Minnesota; and a grant from the National Endowment for the Arts, which believes that a great nation deserves great art. Significant support has also been provided by the Bush Foundation; Target, with support from the Target Foundation; the McKnight Foundation; and other generous contributions from foundations, corporations, and individuals. To these organizations and individuals we offer our heartfelt thanks.

MINNESOTA
STATE ARTS BOARD

NATIONAL
ENDOWMENT
FOR THE ARTS

Published by Graywolf Press
2402 University Avenue, Suite 203
Saint Paul, Minnesota 55114
All rights reserved.

www.graywolfpress.org

Published in the United States of America

ISBN 1-55597-438-4

2 4 6 8 9 7 5 3 1
First Graywolf Printing, 2006

Library of Congress Control Number: 2005932354

Sections of this book have been published in other forms in the *Economist* (bronze medal winner in the Shell/*Economist* 2003 writing competition), *Los Angeles Times Sunday Magazine*, *Mississippi Review* (2005 *Mississippi Review* Prize), and *Zyzzyva*.

Cover design: Kyle G. Hunter
Cover photograph: © Patrik Giardino/CORBIS

For my husband, Dr. Goldstein,
knight errant of the instrumentality
who leads by example
& our daughter,
the dulcet and magical 𝕲𝖆𝖇𝖗𝖎𝖊𝖑𝖑𝖊
who is an outstanding camper.

Contents

In us all it still lives. . . . the dark corners, the secret alleys, shuttered windows, squalid courtyards. . . . the unhealthy old Jewish Town within us.

FRANZ KAFKA

Judge's Statement

A FEW WEEKS AGO AT THE LOCAL LIBRARY fair in New Paltz I found a little book on the fifty-cents table, *English Prose: Wycliffe to Clarendon,* edited by William Peacock. This turned out to be the first of a five-volume set published by Oxford World Classics early in the last century, and reprinted on a few occasions later. The others were easy and almost as inexpensive to track down online. The history of English prose, especially for the early pre-novel volumes, inevitably is also the history of English nonfiction. Some of the writers were variously familiar, at second- if not always firsthand—Malory, Moore, Holinshed, Raleigh, Lyly, Bacon, Nash, Donne, Jonson, Burton, Herbert, Hobbes, Walton, Browne—some completely new to me. But as you worked through the anthology, the parables, histories, prayers, essays, sermons, reminiscences, travels, documents, plays, and letters, you couldn't resist the conclusion that nonfiction once was far more motley, bolder, harder, and stranger than we've come to think of the form over recent decades.

I know of nothing exactly like Kate Braverman's *Frantic Transmissions to and from Los Angeles: An Accidental Memoir,* but I recognize that her book is bold, hard, and strange in the manner of *English Prose: Wycliffe to Clarendon.* *Frantic Transmissions* is foremost a narrative inspirited by space—an anatomy, as it were, of spaces and psyches. Let me propose a miniature tour of some of the spaces—and psyches—inside:

Forty years after their first exposure to the Santa Monica Pier, three women continue to meet up there "at irregular intervals, a birth, a death, a daughter's medical-school graduation, or a chance airline confusion." The women "bear witness," yet the pier, much as their voices joined in song, is only another of L.A.'s "transitory architectures."

An uncle remembers the Jewish villages of Eastern Europe, the tenements of the old East Village. "You might call them pre-Holocaust survivors," as Uncle Irving mordantly tags his family.

Various women tumble into the "limbo of half-lives." Others, luckier or cannier, "vanish." The difference? "After you have vanished, after you have disappeared, after you have found an appropriate and untraceable sublife, you hear what harbors are saying."

A mother and daughter jar applesauce in the kitchen of a farmhouse in the Allegheny Mountains of western New York. "The appeal of this house," the mother guesses, "is that it can't be conventionalized or made more like Los Angeles, not unless we gut and rebuild it."

During a posthumous interview, Marilyn Monroe reveals that "Los Angeles reminds me of children in foster homes at nightfall, when they take their clothes off."

An aunt orders her niece—"the flower child, with the poetry books"—to go away, leave her alone. "Remember," Aunt Sarah says, "you don't have my address."

A real estate agent, showing that New York State farmhouse, informs potential purchasers, "As I mentioned, our sellers are from Los Angeles. During their years of transition from the accumulated atrocities of Southern California, they came to understand, by seasons, by increments of wind howl and fox mew, that the event-horizon landscapes they had internalized are permanent."

"*Space is the most dramatic stylistic entity—from* Giotto *to* Noland, *from* Intolerance *to* Weekend," as film critic and painter Manny Farber once observed. "*How an artist deploys his space. . . .*" Or *her* space, since the radial spaces of Braverman's visionary, devastating book are created or deflected, inherited or disowned, mostly by women. *Frantic Transmissions* dispatches a reckoning of that American space known as Los Angeles; and Braverman might be accounted among the writers and filmmakers in a Southern

California (all but fully male) tradition that spans James M. Cain, Louis Adamic, A. I. Bezzerides, John Fante, Joan Didion, Carey McWilliams, John Rechy, Mike Davis, Gavin Lambert, Walter Mosley, Steve Erickson, D. J. Waldie, James Ellroy, David Thomson, Robert Aldrich, and Robert Altman. But as she notably acknowledges,

> . . . . we did not find our economic, emotional, or physical geography in our assigned English-class novels . . . Los Angeles, the destination city, capital of film and media, did not yet exist . . . We had no monuments . . . no boulevards with bronze statues of poets, composers, or sages on horseback, no museums or artifacts with resonance, no recognizable areas sanctified by American systems of classification . . . We are native daughters of the dirty secret city built around and through and not for us. . . .

Few books prove as sly and resourceful in their memorials of contemporary space (address books and lost childhoods, as well as coasts, farms, and shopping malls), much as few writers manifest Braverman's vigilance to transience, transformation, and repetition, or to the confluences and abrasions of spaces and psyches.

Psyche in the old Greek sense of "breath" inevitably leads back to voice, and *Frantic Transmissions* is also a fierce, elegant medley of voices. Uncle Irving's. Aunt Sarah's. Marilyn Monroe's. The real estate agent's. Letters. Gossip. Boasts. Fears. Chatter. Warnings. Spells. Pitches. Perhaps the signature vocal achievement here is the composite voice of the three woman in Braverman's opening chapter, "Fusion City," at once a stylized abstraction and flexibly particular:

> When I consider my squalid adolescence
> in Los Angeles, it's lit by partial flickers of
> gilded alloys. Sour lemons and citrus leak
> through torn screen-door mesh. Stalled
> glare of a permanent summer like an un-
> diagnosed infection. The core is ochre, the
> distilled essence of abscesses and nicotine.
> And the smell of peroxide on Sundays when
> the mothers prepared for their workweeks,
> pouring bleach on their hair by not enough
> light above stained sinks. They ironed skirts
> and polished their shoes for the buses taking
> them to their jobs as file clerks and secre-
> taries where serving coffee to the boss on a
> tray and removing your skirt went without
> saying.

A memoir? Essays? Kate Braverman is a legendary novelist, short-story writer, and poet, but this book reminds us that nonfiction must be at least as daring and innovative as our strongest poems and novels.

I'm honored to introduce *Frantic Transmissions* as the first recipient of the Graywolf Press Nonfiction Prize.

Robert Polito
New Paltz, New York
July 2005

Fusion City

*W*E MEET AT THE SANTA MONICA PIER AT irregular intervals, a birth, a death, a daughter's medical-school graduation, or a chance airline confusion. Our forty-year friendships are secondary. Memory is not static. It's in flux, mutating through time and accumulation. There's a give, the way cliffs above the Pacific Coast Highway shed themselves across decades. We are left with too few artifacts. Proof is elusive. Sea breezes embrace seductive star jasmine while Santa Anas blow salt through the dusk like stray bullets. But our lives are not fictions. We meet and remember. We bear witness for one another. This is our central function.

There were no simple lines between natural and artificial in our shared youth, though we were aware of these distinctions and how they confused and stained. We were poor and hungry in a mean hardscrabble town that moved with the slow lull of a fishing village. It was the end of the frontier. We had to hang on, inches from the sea. Los Angeles was the last stop before drowning or China or having to learn a new language. It was a gulag with palm trees.

School taught us the value of water, and our precarious position, perched on fault lines and surrounded by desert. We existed by a technological sleight of hand and should be grateful. Of course, our educational opportunities were determined by sociological status. We lived in the already faltering apartments of what would soon be officially recognized and designated as tenements. We wore secondhand clothing. Our mothers worked. The college track was not an option. We were automatically relegated to vocational classes, expected to sew, type, and cook. We were to make curtains, sew hems and seams, and demonstrate proficiency with meat loaf. This was the collective construct of adequate female adult preparation.

No one considered the possibility that we might discipline our minds for endeavors other than serving as wives and secretaries, waitresses and file clerks. Mastery of mathematics and foreign languages was not suggested. We were not expected to transcend our circumstances.

School taught us our mere presence was proof of some version of Manifest Destiny and the demonstration of American scientific prowess. But we did not find our economic, emotional, or physical geography in our assigned English-class novels. Nature was exclusively for the wealthy inhabitants of pastel houses with lawns enclosed by white picket fences, mothers who were full-time housewives, who baked and pruned roses, and family trees that could be traced for generations. Nature was seasons; museums, ballet, stone architecture, rivers, bridges, and last names you recognized instinctively, syllables that when spoken seemed to form church steeples and town squares on your lips.

We had aberrant names like Nakamura and Valdez, Hernandez and Chin. We came from the dust-ruined interiors, spoke with drawls, rented trailers, and it was still the Depression. Neighbors had partial families where blurred photographs attested to the father or daughter still in a wretched Asian port or mud and goat-strewn fetid mountain pueblo. We celebrated the Day of Dead and the Birth of Buddha. We ate with chopsticks and rolled vegetables into tortillas. We did not realize silverware was a regular feature of daily life until we went to college.

Later, we would be labeled latchkey children of dysfunctional families in a still coalescing experiment called Los Angeles. It was the late '50s and our town was stucco tenements planted in rows like the citrus trees we had learned not to eat from. The lemons loitered beside gashes of asphalt alley, the fist-sized oranges like a string of lanterns at eye level and so bitter they burned your mouth.

Los Angeles, the destination city, capital of film and media, did not yet exist. This was an era before the image became holy and ineffable. Our Los Angeles was where you went after divorce and scandal, bankruptcy, foreclosure, imminent starvation, bad health, and personal exile. There was nothing glamorous about it. One came from calamity, lured by the promise of a winter in permanent remission where you could have asthma and heart attacks with a minimal heating bill. It was a plain of divorcees and single mothers. We knew because we babysat for them, observing their covert rites of elaborate preparation for dates where they shed their secretary clothing and wore lipstick, mascara, and tight dresses that sparkled.

Our world was one of stigma and words that could not be uttered. Alcoholism. Cancer. Child abuse. Addiction. Homosexuality. We did not yet possess the vocabulary to define ourselves. But sitting in blistering white sun on Santa Monica Pier, the three of us with our recently invented transistor radios, beginning our afternoon ceremony of searching for discarded glass soda bottles, we knew Holden Caulfield did not have our sort of angst. We hunted empty glass under the pier and redeemed our dangerous harvests for two and three cents apiece, lunch money and if we were fortunate, bus fare back. Home was grim dark boxes beside boulevards where lamps were always required, electricity too expensive, and even the light was rationed.

Here we lived with what would later be called domestic violence, sexual abuse, and mental illnesses that required intervention and psychiatric medication; court-mandated counseling, AA and anger-management support groups. In short, Holden Caulfield would have taken a taxi.

The definitions of cities were obvious and inviolate. And we didn't apply. We had no monuments or subways, no boulevards with bronze statues of poets, composers, or sages on horseback, no museums or artifacts with resonance, no recognizable areas sanctified by American systems of classification. All Los Angeles could do was grow in an ungainly manner, sprawl it was called, implying the drunken and misshapen. We were innately defective. The heroines we encountered in literature experienced insight and revelation while carrying umbrellas, further shaping our conviction that culture and dampness were inexorably connected. We didn't even have rain.

Los Angeles was, from inception, already decaying. It was a city of subtle psychological apartheid, of them and us. We who actually lived here, and the others, who might come if lured. Our dwellings were designed for transience. Apartments without dining rooms, as if anticipating a future where families disintegrated, compulsively dieted or ate alone, in front of televisions. Smog and the intricate residues of a human misery no one named hung thick above a drab geometry of squat substandard buildings in rows. It was an aggressive linearity designed for people who would be spending their decades in lines, identified by number, rather than name. We were the first sketch of the welfare state, Sunbelt style.

They claimed to be building a highway across burlap brown bean fields behind our alley to connect Los
Angeles to San Diego. It was probably a rumor, like
stories of movie stars living in a place called Malibu.
Even if true, such a road was irrelevant. San Diego
was farther than we would ever be able to walk.
Nature was what happened when you walked out
your door. Or was it? We were denied maples and
oaks, the deciduous trees that obeyed the European
natural order of budding, spring, summer, and the incomprehensible illumination of an autumn of leaves
turning yellow and red, burgundy and orange before
the ordained winter. Our nature was what pushed
up on its own accord from slats in fences and cracks
in alleys, the blaze of crimson and gold canna, the
sticky white and pink oleander, sudden eruptions of
agapanthus and jacaranda. Our nature was innumerable varieties of palm trees that were not deciduous
but unrepentantly vertical, with pitiful daggers of
unpredictable partial shade. Holden Caulfield would
have stabbed himself.

We didn't know we would be revised and labeled
the prototype global village. We knew what we could
walk and our anomalous caste. Streets named Pacific,
Pico, Loma Vista, Sepulveda, and La Cienega assured us we were different and inferior. The disenfranchised, condemned to the shabby festering like
burn sores remains of what had been built to accommodate WWII soldiers. The boys shipping out to the

wars in Asia who vowed to return with young wives to the orange groves by the ocean and did. It was the minimal architecture of pragmatism, conformity, and greed, in the pseudo-tropical fashion that became the blueprint for the new slums in the sun. I was there. I was the penciled-in stick figure in the schematics.

These were the virtual tropics, with a Mexican rhythm and an Oakie beat. We inhabited a not American terrain, air a score of palm fronds, shoulder-high orange hibiscus, ridges of bamboo navigated by nuances of unremitting summer beside walls decomposing beneath a radiant colossus of magenta bougainvillea there were no poems about. Finally, after miles of alleys and avenues wearing the unexpected names of Spanish saints and generals, the bay at Santa Monica, pale as if bleached by acid. Our brothers fished for bonito, bass, and halibut. There were still fish in Santa Monica Bay, and you could eat them without fear of lethal poisoning.

Now we meet at random occasions, forty years later, always at the Pier. The water in winter is blue as delphiniums and larkspur. In spring, it's the cerulean ink you might employ for a love letter, sanctified, electric, and graceful. The waters form their own morphologies and hierarchies. The fall bay is like a visa stamp or fading tattoo. Then the pause before sunset when everything is veiled in azure. You hear what could be bells from a ship or cathedral, but you can't be certain. Waves suggest rain, dream and hallucination. And you realize there is no actual line between drowning and communion. Or what is natural versus artificial. Do we not reinvent ourselves from our personal rubble? Is the human drama itself not that of inspired nonlinear transformation? Usually the bay is listless, waves so light and restrained they're merely theoretical, like a gauzy fluid you could wrap a cut in. It's a defeated blue, depressed and contained. It looks like it's on Prozac. Still, there is a startled quality in this breeze, some seaport implication of vessels sunken by storms, holds filled with plundered gold crowns and stolen statues of someone else's gods. And ships with mysterious cargoes of millennial contraband, computer chips, girls with forged documents, and the opiates and jewels men have smuggled and bartered for 8,000 years. In such vessels antiquities and powders are hidden, and residues with viruses from pigs, birds, and monkeys in unpronounceable cities. But wasn't it always this way? The fear of disease, the intuitive logic of why we stoned the wandering stranger?

The three of us, bearing witness on the Santa Monica Pier, breathing sea dust, a fragrance that might be a fusion of perfumed oils, opium, cayenne, sandalwood, and wind. The ocean is continuous. In the becalmed suspension before sunset, waves break in lines like fingers, or the multiple arms of ancient deities. We have six arms. We sing songs from our transistor-radio summers. I consider the way prayers are intoned, how the human voice insinuates itself in air and forms elegant, transitory architectures. Perhaps these are the lost cities men are incessantly seeking, in rain forests and electron microscopes, beneath reefs and in biochemical recombination. Today we meet in heat and its inevitabilities. Haze on the vaguely Mediterranean hills like a cursed Greece perhaps, stalled in their own fouled pastels. Mutation is in the sky, an ambiguous caress of subtle fragrant toxins lacerating the air. Palms on cliffs seem to take a breath, as if preparing for sordid evening, the glare preceding the contaminated lavenders.

Then sun sets in an orange so aggressively hard and metallic, it is shocking. If you looked directly at it, you could become scarred. It's a sunset that makes me think of knives and car crashes and having my face reconstructed on the basis of photographs. We couldn't be identified by our dental records. We didn't have dentists. That would have been a luxury.

We had appliances: garbage disposals, refrigerators, and telephones. They came standard-issue with our standard-issue apartments, but we had stringent regulations about using them. Garbage disposals were viewed as elaborate ecosystems. Who knew what could be spewed out? Bone chips, metallic pellets, acids that caused contagions like tuberculosis and encephalitis. Who knew what was in such pipes? We turned it on and ran from the room, shielding our eyes, hoping shrapnel wouldn't lodge in our backs. It wasn't an appliance. It was a war zone.

As for the telephone, it shouldn't even be touched. It was the time of toll calls. The cow town at the edge of the implausible ocean was divided into area codes. Calls within your own zone were free. Each outer region had a progressive cost associated with it. We had telephones. We just weren't allowed to look at them.

Behind us are the once-derelict canals of Venice, ducks drifting slow on lyrical waterways in front of seven-figure shacks flanked by embankments of seared red geraniums. Jacaranda is in metamorphosis. Hibiscus is molting. And the constant siege of flowering South American vines against garages and porches that look too frail to contain them.

We are indigenous. We believe instinctively in ambushes and guerilla actions, here where palms lean windswept and brazen. Farther inland, women stand in plazas, exposed in light mist remnants of dusks like powdered lilacs. They lean from tiny terraces, their mouths form shapes you cannot decipher, and their lips turn night pewter. It is for this vertigo that we travel.

Now the Ferris wheel on the pier is neon pink, an electric calligraphy simultaneously tawdry and alluring. Alchemy always promised such marriages of vulgarity and enchantment. As women of port cities have always done, we have sampled the wares these trade routes brought. Between us, we have amassed nearly a century of psychotherapy, decades of graduate school, cycles of promiscuity and celibacy, yoga, rehab, relapse, AA, politics and activism. We have learned the difference between pastimes and actual skills. We have acquired the information necessary to garden, sail, play guitar and flute, ski, scuba dive, speak and read four languages. We have climbed the Great Wall of China, sat at the feet of the Sphinx, stood at the Wailing Wall, toured the Taj Mahal, Borodor, Blue Mosque, and beaches of Fiji and Bora Bora. We collect latitudes and longitudes the way other women might property and stock. This is our evidence, our proof. We communicate by postcards.

We meet between Bombay and Bali. After we psychologically removed the sting of the slap across the cheek and the split lip, which took decades of therapy, we went further. We surgically removed the jowls of our fathers. We have cheekbones and chins. When we look in the mirror, we no longer see the faces of the biological entities that called us trash and stupid sluts. We purchased porcelain crowns to encase feral yellow teeth that never saw orthodontists. Lasers took our facial hair, astigmatisms, and varicose veins. We discovered our bones, shed the protective unnecessary flesh, and exercise to retain our willed-into-existence forms.

Is this the artificiality one immediately associates

with Los Angeles? Or is this a singular and deliberate sequence of acts of directed personal evolution?

We are native daughters of the dirty secret city built around and through and not for us. We are what coalesced at the end of the trail after the bandits, dust, cactus, and coyotes. We clawed out of the flawed operation, trial-and-error hybrids that still breathe. We did not live in the Puritan dark forest of Hawthorne with an evil and dangerous environment to subdue. We were not in conflict with our version of nature and coexisted with its boldly exquisite eccentricities. Our assumptions were modernistic; distance, travel, and impermanence were givens. We recognized our adulthoods would not be limited by static geography or accidents of birth but volitional borders created by aesthetics and affinities.

We are the spawn of hillsides of succulents stirring under relentless sun. We have lived like our city, as flagrant works in progress. We stand on Santa Monica Pier, in the landscape of childhood, with the carousel spinning in primary colors, vivid and pulsating. It's our original neon alphabet, and we are small and awed again. It is before proportion, corruption, gridlock, drive-by shootings, heartbreak, and mortality. It is the world of childhood and dream where coherence is not required, one drifts between images, and gravity is intermittent.

Should we have survived our circumstances? It was not chance, but acts of discipline, intuition, intelligence, and courage that brought us from smeared windows with sliced views of wire fences bordering freeways, cement banks littered by pieces of broken baby carriages and bent toys. It is behind us, the miniature balconies with geraniums decaying in tin cans in air soiled from chemical fumes and human wounds one did not speak about.

When I consider my squalid adolescence in Los Angeles, it's lit by partial flickers of gilded alloys. Sour lemons and citrus leak through torn screen-door mesh. Stalled glaze of a permanent summer like an undiagnosed infection. The core is ochre, the distilled essence of abscesses and nicotine. And the smell of peroxide on Sundays when the mothers prepared for their workweeks, pouring bleach on their hair by not enough light above stained sinks. They ironed skirts and polished their shoes for the buses taking them to jobs as file clerks and receptionists where serving coffee to the boss on a tray and removing your skirt went without saying. The City of the Angels as she was, before sexual harassment was designated politically incorrect and slapping your wife across the face wasn't an acceptable punctuation.

We are middle age. We have buried husbands, parents, and siblings. We have mortgages and contract disputes, agents, lawyers, accountants, personal trainers, and financial managers. Our children are ballet dancers, scientists, and architects. Between us, we have dental implants, hearing aids, contact lenses, breast enhancements, face-lifts, and hip replacements. We are taking chemotherapy treatments, hormones, hypertension and diabetes medicines, tranquilizers, antidepressants, and smoking pot. Are we evolving toward cyborgs? Are we becoming some biochemical and technologically modified and enhanced version of our original selves? We hope so.

We stand at the end of the pier. The marginalized devise unique rituals of solace and achievement. From this pier, we have cast off wedding rings and tossed documents and photographs of those who betrayed us. When you are a girl child of anonymous asphalt crevices and gullies, you invent what is consigned to the sea, what constitutes corruption and resurrection. Between us, we've seen more than Cleopatra and Helen of Troy. We possess the systematic perspective they could not have known. We recognize it is a rare alchemy of pollution that turns sunset into strata of intoxication, strands like sherry, brandy, and wine. We know why the sky seems smeared with iodine and saffron.

Between us we have six arms, like Shiva and Kali. We sway our multiple limbs in an instinctive sequence ancient before the Sirens. We don't need an iPod. We know this choreography. We are women of the wharves and rocks, seducing the frayed night with our flesh, telepathically commanding ships to crash.

Weren't there always witches and shamen, adepts and anomalies? Doesn't mythology demonstrate human metamorphosis as intrinsic and the forms of civilization to be in constant transition? Weren't there always treasures and portents? Women skilled with augury and clairvoyance?

This night jacaranda on bluffs behind us open like lilac mouths, promising a hot kiss. The ocean is a corridor of violet-tinted mirrors that lead everywhere. We understand the elements. We smell and hear the moon. But we must be quick. One of us has a plane to catch, just south of the pier, in the sheered belly that cuts like a scalpel through the archive of stars.

Escaping Los Angeles: Incantations and Magic

*Y*OU DON'T JUST LEAVE LOS ANGELES. Such a departure requires magical intervention. You can't simply purchase a ticket to another destination. You must disappear.

This is how to vanish. It's a process with a mutable formula. It's like a recipe.

First, envision an unusual city above a harbor or inland, surrounded by fields of barley and potatoes. It is a sky of martyrs and kidnapping. Perhaps you remember an island, Ibiza, say, the July and August before graduate school. You went to the bakery, the store with cheeses, stands with fruit, and the late afternoon fish market. You were supposed to be studying Spanish. But you didn't. You filled a net shopping bag with items procured in a motion so slow, a choreography so arrested, it seemed to be happening to someone else. One pear, one mango, one melon, one pale onion at each juncture. Then it was dusk. At night you slept with strangers.

Now you understand your miscalculation, the strained equation, how you thought degrading your flesh would make you disappear. Now you suspect

Ibiza was your first flawed attempt to vanish. Women often convince themselves certain landscapes are a permanent revelation. It's a common mistake. Don't make it again.

A true disappearance requires a radical new geography, vegetation, and seasons. For instance, you might come from Los Angeles, where sea breezes mix salty citrus and sand in the air like metal pellets. Los Angeles, when it was the end of the line, when it was exile. Apartments nailed in rows beside gashes of cement alley. Boulevard sounds were abrupt moans and corrupt, tainted metallic spasms. No woman or dog could howl like that, like some creature of rumor strangling on razored garbage. You were expected to get used to it.

Because the heroines of novels you read in your youth discovered illumination while walking in rain, your vanishing requires constant thunderstorms in a province of pewter above plazas of stained silver. It is 6 p.m. over and over. The somber hour of cathedral bells plying their meager trade through rain. You are immune. You have no remorse and acres of unmolested silence.

These are suggestions, outlines, maps that indicate where the swamps and mountain ranges are, the routes of bandits and slave traders who specialize in women and girl children. How you cross continents of desert, construct vessels for rivers and inland seas, resist disease, invent camouflage and weapons are individual matters.

It might serve to memorize the habits of deciduous trees. Forests nourish and protect. Select a maple as a role model. It will be a better mother than the one who birthed you, believe me. Later, you develop navigational skills, remember not street names, which are subject to arbitrary alteration, but rather that your dwelling is four boulevards beyond the park with its statue of a horse-mounted soldier famous for his stamina and half-century innovative torture regime. You've seen the bronze general ringed by eleven chestnuts. He's a reference point.

It may take years to learn where to buy pumpernickel, almond croissants, how to find fresh sole and lamb, and the methods for procuring pears. There's the matter of who sometimes offers mangoes or papayas. Such stores come into possession of the tropical without warning, randomly, crates arrive in the night like contraband. Then an inconspicuous hand-printed sign in the window. The vanished are fluent with such calligraphy.

"What are you thinking?" he will ask.

"Oh," you are permitted one partial sigh. You are a crescent moon screened by clouds. It's a sky to hide in. You must say, "Nothing."

It is imperative you do not reveal your rudimentary plans, your first sketches of disappearance. The void is a confluence of streetlamp ambers the trade winds brought and hallways lit by fathers smoking, cigarettes secret citadels in the dark, an invitation. Your early strategies are vulnerable. A glance could shatter them. You could experience vertigo, forget the emerging grid and where to jump. You could become an old woman in a wicker rocker on a porch, making a list of the chances she missed, pushing thick air with gnarled fingers through a soiled paper fan. A generic-aged woman who seems to be trying to reconstruct something specific, like locations and coordinates.

This old woman is framing a single question. What do vanished people know? This is simple. The vanished know holidays are important, and they have memorized each one. They are the periphery, after all. They are like you were in Los Angeles, perhaps, beyond the boundary, deep within a crevice of starched pink hibiscus. Such women swell crowds on the Fourth of July. They are the reason for parades and the ritual slaughter of baby pines. There could be no decorations, no holly wreaths or mutilated pumpkins without them. This is why girls are taught the dance of the maypole ribbons. They are instructed in this particular weaving in fifth grade, and they never forget.

The disappeared memorize all shortcuts. They possess an intuition for the physical world, realize that jogging a quarter of a mile of cobblestone passageway and climbing sixty unexpected stone steps is faster than thirty minutes in a taxi. The disappeared know where the carvings are, the buried frescoes and shrines thought lost to sand and jungle. They often live there. They also know where stolen museum paintings and submerged ships are. The sound of waves across rotting wood and gold is specific and unmistakable, like a beacon.

Once women vanish, they acquire an instinct for fragrances. They become adept at the conjunction of scent and skin, the gradations between bronze and peach, and have lotions and perfumes made to order. They design the proportions, two parts vanilla, say, and a trace of musk, cinnamon, patchouli, almond, honey, and lilac. This is just an example.

They comprehend liquid measurements, and what they imply. They practice with transparent fluids such as white wine, vodka, absinth, and gin. They are precise in their acquisitions, which shade of mauve silk scarf is required, what style leather gloves. They determine the correct shape of pocketbooks the way ordinary women select ripe melons. They simply hold them up to the light and are immediately certain. They receive tactile cues they accommodate and synthesize. Their fingers are flawless conductors. When a woman disappears, there is no deformity or arthritis, no loss of balance, tumors, disease, vacillation, or indecision. There are no mistakes.

The intricacies of geography become trivial. They sense incipient trade routes as they emerge, ports and villages and where to vacation and purchase real estate. It is obvious. Costa Rica, Istanbul, Prague. And something rocky and gray with mist and moss off Scotland that doesn't yet have a name.

"You look so intent," the man might say. Not words but a mesh, nets, traps. He's been working on his arrow points for two million years. He can pound, sharpen, and whittle.

"I'm just listening," you may answer, eyes downcast, voice soft. Clouds have shielded the sky with titanium. No moon.

"To what?" he will ask. He is pressing you. This is chess, football, and combat, simultaneously.

"Oh," this is a moment for improvisation. You might risk letting your eyes briefly meet. "To the stars and owls. To the night."

Disappearing women are consumed with the auditory. Plazas and cathedrals, foghorns and bells, form sequences, like points of light that can be plotted on a graph. There are implications in scraping pigeons and the stooped and shawled women feeding them breadcrumbs in deserted parks surrounded by denuded oaks and lindens.

There is the matter of the faces of women in apartment windows, smoking cigarettes, drying aprons on black iron rails, in angular patches of frail November sun. This is legible to vanishing women like a script, a text. Such women have blue eyes and a parakeet in a cage, plastic covering the good sofa where they never sit, and photographs of grandchildren taped to kitchen cupboards. These women do not even glance at these pictures. They could be anyone's grandchildren. They might be faxed in from distant planets. They have nothing to do with them, or the harbor and courtyards, the trolleys and bridges and birds in their northern or southern formations, where they go, what they do, why they wail and shriek.

Once a woman disappears she instinctively knows the names and histories of strangers. She recognizes kinship to all women standing on terraces or sitting alone on bus benches and porches. But adepts make distinctions. Women with birds in cages and regular mail delivery have lost their coordinates. Their vanishing is incomplete. That's the difference, the variable of state, and what a vanishing woman in training must avoid.

This is an essential ingredient like a flour sifter or oven thermometer. Remember, most women are failures. They flirted with vanishing, they conceived of it, but lacked the stamina and imagination to construct the tunnels or devices to scale the fences. They could not devise spontaneous dialogue and postures to deceive the border guards, the radar. They did not comprehend how to procure forged documents, who to bribe, blackmail, or kill. They weren't ruthless and prepared.

They didn't carry a 9-mm with hydro-shock bullets. They didn't learn martial arts or hike with a

60-lb. backpack through the Sangre de Cristo for five weeks, finding creeks not on maps and cutting cactus for water. Instead, their shadows leaked out of them. Their dreams were reduced to only black and white. All that remained was a triangle of diminished autumn sun and bells in an abstract distance that mean less than a vague prolonged punctuation. These women inhabit the periphery of neighborhoods where languages they do not understand are spoken. They have become women of the backwater ports. Creatures of cul-de-sacs. They inhabit a realm like a coma and breathe through invisible life-support machines. Don't go there.

It is possible to distinguish women who have successfully vanished. They are often drawn to smoke. They are not afraid of fire. They consume two or three packages of cigarettes a day. They have red lacquers applied to their fingernails. They inhale Temple Ball opium from antique glass and cloisonné pipes once used by concubines. They paint their mouths vermilion. The spectrum of flame is their friend. They write with quill pens and gold ink. They are not anxious at twilight or in the awkward settling of hour and season, the ragged gap before the lamps are lit.

When a woman disappears there are few mysteries. The face is a composition. They know exactly how to evaluate subtle variances between rose blushes, cinnamon and coral orchid. It's a physical sensation, a heat skin seeks or avoids. The gradations and nuances are distinct as musical notes. No errors. The vanished have the fingers of a surgeon, a concert pianist.

They often possess an instinct for which gifts to purchase. They are no longer bewildered or frustrated in department stores by a profusion of too many sweaters, by a barrage of patterns and materials. It is always an occasion for gray, charcoal, and black cashmere, and camel coats. Vanished women are more intimate with these objects, their specific manifestations and what they demand, than they were with past husbands.

Vanished women are fluent in French and Italian. They are familiar with the languages of opera and those of antiquity, Greek, Hebrew, and Coptic. The Cyrillic alphabet has a particular appeal. They crave scripts that appear only on coins in museum display cases. They open such cabinets by the force of their will. They cause the guards to turn away, such is their influence. Then they slide the coins into their purse, trace the faces of dead princes and butcher presidents through gloved fingers. They possess an intricate Braille. Networks of neurons spark in their coat pocket. They carry stolen antiquities that feel like secret embers, explosives, the final expression of a process that began with flint.

It's a perpetual autumn. Leaves are a litany of kissed mouths in gutters. The maples will be lantern yellow and fever red until the moon drops dead. They have internal adjustments to monitor. Vanished women take potions for hunger, insomnia, and nerves. Such remedies are procured by exchanges in moonlit alleys and barter under night bridges where one must be fluent in the dialects of contraband.

Vanished women do not require specific love. They are never lonely. How could they be, with the air unraveling like a text they possess a gift to decipher? They have intuition and diligence. Often they open shops for fortune-telling. They build a clientele addicted to their crystal ball, the patterns it casts across a face. They determine by scent who has ovarian cancer, who will die by heart seizure or broken glass. Vanished women know the truth but lie. For women, the Fifth Amendment is the only survival clause.

They walk boulevards, their progress a sequence of subtle elations culminating in a noon so lucid and indelible they feel they are being scarred. They must shield their faces with hats and partial veils.

Soon, all abnormalities become tolerable. They accommodate toxins and disappointment with ease. Some carry a parasol and keep curtains closed during sun days. There is nothing to see below but the tinny tease of maples, the filigree antique gold coating leaves with an intoxicating rust. They stay in bed, memorizing names of extinct seas and flowers in their many languages. They do not need books to acquire knowledge. It comes through an entirely other process, a separate channel. They recite syllables of the sacred dead, and rooms fill with invisible origami. These are accidental prayers made visible. These are the unexpected shrines that hang like strands of ivy or party decorations along walls only other disappeared women see. They suspect the dead are actually vanished, removed from the ordinary grid. The crypts are empty. Heaven is an alias and a false address.

Vanished women have extrasensory perception and never sunburn. They know which stocks to buy and when to sell. It's like a biorhythm. Or learning how to decipher dreams, which are simply acres encased in obvious crypto-religious symbology. They have the key for uncoding.

Occasionally, one can recognize vanished women at racetracks where they are prophetic with horse betting. They select gray mares with autumn names containing rain and bridges in them, ports and drowned men. Names with rivers and blues that evoke fluid demarcations. Vanished women are discreet and carry in their leather purses stacks of cash, Euros, American, and Yuan. They wear boots because they prefer walking. It's the only way to become intimate with a city. You must kiss each brick, each cobblestone with your feet. When your soles bleed and you must bandage yourself each morning, you realize you are getting somewhere.

When a woman vanishes, everything is intelligible, human motivations and what wires carry. All impulses are equally coherent and predictable. Once a woman divests herself of the ordinary, a procedure often requiring metal cutting tools and amputation, and can be done with a penknife or teeth if necessary, she becomes more than subterranean. Then are the acts of reconstruction, one atom at a time. Afterward, they know which books to read, films to view, and the significant gallery openings. They know which numbers to play, that 44 and 47 are for roulette and any of the 40s are for the lottery. They order with ease in restaurants and cafés, intuitively selecting the best entrée and what isn't listed on the menu. They wear a hat with a veil, request delicacies in a whisper, accent impeccable. No one could refuse them.

"I feel you're far away," the man might say. He is observing you, calculating, forming equations he may take to a representative of the patriarchy, such as a doctor, lawyer, or military official. He is considering physical incarceration and/or biochemical imprisonments such as occur with antidepressants. He is dangerous.

This is a juncture where you may smile. This is optional. You might allow your lips to form the ambiguous seductive shape of slow regret. Or let your mouth fill with too much night, incinerated maple leaves and fox teeth. "Not really," you may answer. What you mean is, *not yet.*

It occurs to you that not only vanished women

live this way. For instance, everything is always in season for missing children, for miscarried, aborted, runaway, and murdered children. They are not gone. They are riding cruise ships in the Caribbean. Islands are dots they connect with their relentless passage. It is tropical with plumeria, coconuts, and wind in green waves. When you are a vanished woman or child, you can buy gardenias, dahlias, and peonies any day of the year, even on winter-thunderstorm Sundays.

When a disappeared woman reemerges, when she has reassembled herself on a molecular level, she returns with a tattoo of a blue crescent moon on her neck or a cluster of hearts on her thigh. She procures passports in the names of jewels and fragrant flowers. Camellia, Jade, Rose, Iris, Ruby, Hyacinth. She lists her occupation as student. She says she is self-employed.

Skin changes with the seasons, particularly if you have disappeared with a violent severing. This is why one must strive for small methodical points of exit. One doesn't want to make a scene. One doesn't want them burning candles in the windows. Such gestures and their glare give the vanished migraines.

When a woman has vanished with the simple elegance of smoke, she discovers her eyes alter at will. In winter, she wears the spectrum of bruises, violets, lavenders, and grays. Her eyes are coal and sapphire. In spring, she is all manifestations of pink, sheen of burgundy, and the vestiges of ruined wines. She wears floral prints and frosted lipsticks like a girl. She is fifteen again and smells of too much tea rose. In summer, her skin tans, eyes go green, and she wears burnt auburn. Vanished women cannot resist heated bronze and gold. They wear necklaces of heavy metals that are not costume jewelry. In an anomaly of Indian summer, their hair turns red. They remove their veils, wear white straw hats and thin. They live like plants fed directly by sun. They are rooted in air like certain orchids.

Then fall again, and everything is silver. Autumn lacks a border, elongates. Vanished women know it is winter when their hair turns raven. It continues to rain. Their skin is translucent, the arteries in their arms pulse. The morphine cruising their veins looks like purple neon. When ordinary people chance to see this, they think of rivers and boulevards and borders crossed by deception. If a vanished woman spoke, she might tell them this is how to drown standing up.

Few hear vanished women, or see the temporary bodies they inhabit. They belong only to autumn, hats with feathers and veils, constant storms and cigarette smoke. Vanished women have affection for the way autumn is punctured and lays at their feet like a cloak of blue fox. Shadows collect in rooms where they are quietly reading poetry out loud in Spanish or Italian. If someone were to unexpectedly enter, the intruder would fall to the floor, stunned, thinking only of bridges across ancient rivers, the Euphrates and Nile most particularly. The stranger would leave by ambulance, consumed by images from folklore known only by intuition and rumor.

Vanished women are aquatinted with all forms of subterfuge. They can turn their eyes the color of tragedy, granite gray, a two-pit quarry enormous like a primitive winter ocean before seashells and barter. The translation: Don't even think about it. No one gets across.

"Do you want to go to bed?" he will ask. This is inevitable.

"OK," you may answer. Any syllables will do. It is imperative to utter words like charms. You offer verbal amulets, milagros of knives, hearts, and corncobs, but it is essential your body does not move. You must envision anchors, wooden trunks on the floor of the North Atlantic Ocean, and how large buildings are, with their concrete roots.

Once you have vanished, autumn camouflages you. Weather defines your moods, your physical appearance, the way your hair can go from flame red to ash during the course of one sudden brutal thought. If someone spoke with urgency, surprising you, your eyes and teeth might both fall out.

There must be no intrusion. Remember, you have no fear of bridges, transition, sickness, or the subconscious. You know the names of every tree, what each slain emperor did. You can recite battles and statistics, the exact location of events and their harvest of body bags. You are familiar with the history of agriculture and the way cities formed, often near rivers. You determine which dynasty a vase came from with a single partial glance. You can do this through the mesh of your veil.

After you have vanished, after you have disappeared, after you have found an appropriate and untraceable sublife, you hear what harbors are saying. You sense which coasts to trust, which waves, which lullabies, which pale blue litanies. You decipher currents effortlessly. You know what they bring. Thursday was mangoes. Wednesday, a string of amber and red garnets, two punctured tires, a colossus of clamshells, parts of an umbrella and cello. Perhaps tomorrow will be kelp in strands like helixes, rib cages, and wheels from oxcarts or bicycles.

Crinoline, taffeta, chiffon. This is what vanished daughters wear. Their disappeared mothers prefer velvet and tweed, grays, cuff trim the texture of shadow. There are no dead women. The bodies laid in boxes dressed for parties have nothing to do with who they were or are now. Ridiculous, those three-dimensional fading afterthoughts. Your mother. Your daughter. The women you loved are merely disappeared from the consensual version, walking in handcrafted leather boots through legendary cities, buying loaves of brown bread and pears.

"We should talk," the man might say. He's taking out the bait now, the lures, hooks and sinkers.

"Not now." This is when you must refuse.

It is of utmost importance that you do not lose pieces of yourself before your vanishing is complete. You must avoid gratuitous acts of unborn geography. I know this for a fact. I know a woman, she was a writer, yes. I admit this. A poet from Los Angeles. She once planned to move to Portland. She spoke with her husband about a brick house on a hill, leaded-glass windows, long months of rain, a room with a piano and skylights.

This woman embraced Portland with a shocking affection. For an entire arrested autumn the rain would be silver and specific. The air would be distilled. She would keep it in a crystal decanter. They spent midnights, this husband and wife, living in the house that did not exist in the city where they did not move.

Later, this same woman imagined herself in a farmhouse in Pennsylvania. Her husband said they would have a trout stream, sixty acres, a glass shed for growing poppies and orchids, a pair of German shepherds. They would order them in white, if that breed were as big and smart as the other. They would talk, this husband and his wife, about the flagrant autumn, the siege of inflamed leaves turning henna, burgundy, and claret. They would sleep ringed by apple trees. She could almost hear them singing through their scorched red mouths. But then they didn't move there, either.

I know that woman. Trust me. She is there in some partial life, with the white German shepherds. She is there with the trout stream and farm that never happened and she is locked in stasis, trapped between sublives, imprisoned. Some women build their own concentration camps, their own archipelagos. They string the barbed wire. They dig the lime pits.

Alternatively, this woman is on a hill in Portland. She can never descend because she has no legs. That part of her body is walking through glazed maples in Pennsylvania. Her legs are disembodied and restless, encrusted with rashes such as the bedridden have after years in back wards where no one has touched them since Christmas inspection, and the sheets have merged with the fibers of their flesh.

This particular woman, the case in point, is in a limbo of half-lives. It is always raining, but this woman hasn't managed to vanish. She fell for the just give me one more chance, the take one glance from the balcony at Amalfi, say, or Tahiti. Just look with me for a moment, how can it hurt? Then the chat about analysis and the laws of thermodynamics. The one 3.2 carat diamond ring thing, the just one baby thing. Maybe she permitted them to pry open her mouth and deposit the current approved medicine that washes the color off inside, and then they don't have to build more prisons. You bake apple pies for the next six years and call it living.

The details vary. It's that moment when you lose your aim, become convinced of magic tricks, that beautiful women can be sawed in half on theater tables and immediately restored, and that there are methods for extracting rabbits from hats. They call these manifestations of civilization and acts of love.

Now I'll tell you the absolute truth. This woman hasn't disappeared. She's made herself a paraplegic. She's in a locked ward where they keep the severed women in wheelchairs with soiled khaki army blankets across their withering laps. She hasn't vanished. This particular woman is lost.

Escaping Los Angeles: Uncle Irving's Advice

*Y*OU WANT TO LEAVE LOS ANGELES? What are you, crazy? You got a place to stay with a roof. You don't need an overcoat here. The whole world wants to come to L.A. and you want to leave?

Listen. Remember your background. Look at the big picture. See, I grew up Jewish. Sure it was New York and different. But we weren't the classic Jews you hear about. Read about. The endorsed version. That's the story of how they leap off the ship in Ellis Island. Then the father works twenty hours a day. He's a tailor. He goes blind so his son can be a neurosurgeon or conduct the Boston Symphony. The father, call him Marvin, keeps sewing. He's completely blind at this point, but has to put the son through med school. His hands are like a bloated cactus. The old man looks like a Joshua tree in a brutal decade in a parched century when you open your mouth and sand blows in and nobody remembers what rain is. But in those days, that was considered honorable. It was a triumph. That was politically correct then.

But not everybody climbed out of steerage and

started strategically placing their children in position for graduate school. The standard stumbling back to the tenement stuff you hear about. Walking in snow, of course, to save nickels and dimes. They didn't have a concept of discretionary spending. They treated coins with the awe and respect of relics recovered from excavated tombs. Decades of digging in rock and finally you hold the cool gold orb with the face of a king known only by rumor in your palm. In those days, it wasn't spare change. It was an artifact.

Then climbing steep unlit steps up to the tenement. The kids are doing their third or fourth set of optional extra-credit book reports by candlelight. They're memorizing the next three weeks' spelling lists while practicing the violin. The mother is watching. Call her Sophie. She can't speak English yet, but can intuit a spelling mistake by some form of telepathy. She knows how long violin practice lasts. She doesn't need a watch. It goes until you have carpel tunnel syndrome. When the fingers have neuropathy and paralyze into fused claws, you blow the candle out. That's a normal night.

OK. The old almost blind tailor, Marvin, and his wife are ready for the marital night ritual. And it wasn't sex. Who had strength? It was a verbal tenderness.

"Marvin, what do you think? A dentist?" Sophie closes her eyes in a kind of passion. "Those hands. Marvin, the fingers of a violinist, a cardiologist?"

Marvin embraces her in darkness. That's because

it's freezing in there and the only candle is in the room where the boys do homework. "I think brain surgery," Marvin says.

"Brain surgery," Sophie repeats. "Brain surgery." They say it in unison and it's like the Jewish version of an orgasm.

But not everyone fell asleep to that litany. That's the official version, the laminated 3″ × 5″ image. It's got as much to do with reality as a postcard from Los Angeles showing a coast like French Polynesia with reefs and translucent green lagoons. Sun sets red and purple on top of palm trees that look like no dust, insult, or smog ever touched them. Yeah, maybe it looked like that one day in another century if you were stationed in precisely the right coordinates for thirty seconds. Then they airbrushed out the rotting shacks, gangsters in cars doing drive-by shootings, the garbage washing up from the toxic bay with anemic waves like a sixth-round chemo IV drip, the fish so bloated with mercury they explode while you reel them in.

The truth is, some immigrants didn't just leap off the ships. Our relatives refused to leave. They thought steerage was a good deal. They had a roof, so what if it was canvas? Walls and a few blankets. They had a collection of what the soon-to-be blind tailors left behind. Some old coats, a scarf a woman dropped. When the rest of the passengers ran out for Ellis Island, objects fell from bundles and packs.

Somebody had to gather them. My people didn't need to hold a caucus. They quietly volunteered. They had a locket, shawls, maybe watches.

Actually, our ancestors were evicted from the ships. They didn't enthusiastically march into immigration. They crawled off. Dazed. Subliterate in Russian, in Polish, barely speaking Yiddish. They knew curses and how to ask for credit and bread. Our group stayed after the rats left. They suspected something was happening, but they adopted a neutral position. Let's wait and see. Look, we've got a pile of glass bracelets, three belts, another framed photograph. Could be copper or bronze. We still have the crackers those suckers left. We'll stay. See, they thought it was a treasure hunt.

They didn't get out of steerage until police physically removed them. Then did they get a cart and start hawking rags and potatoes like they were supposed to? No. These people staggered through Ellis Island and they interviewed badly. If it was an audition, they wouldn't have gotten a callback. Name? City of departure? They couldn't come up with plausible fill-in-the-forms, get stamped, and keep-the-paper-moving answers. They had complexities and ambiguities that didn't fit on standard documents. They were too neurotic to just give a name and country. If the bureaucracy worked, they would have sent them back. Free passage in the return direction. No forms. Just go now. I'll tell you something. They didn't have Homeland Security then any more then they have it now.

Our relatives spent a generation walking in listless circles. Ruthie says, "Saul, where am I?"

Saul says, "I don't know."

Ruthie says, "Saul, what are we going to do? Where do we go? What are those machines? Trains? Buses? How do we get on? Are there stairs? Are those seats?"

Saul says, "Ruthie, am I God? Do I know?"

You have to understand the sociology. There were a great variety of Jews. A whole spectrum. You've seen the *Time* magazine covers? Three men who changed the century? Three Jews. Einstein, Freud, and Marx. My people never heard of these guys. They were the horde established and acculturated Jews were trying to keep trapped in the old country. Romania. Poland. Czechoslovakia. Russia. They wanted to commission private companies to build fences and ditches to restrain them. The real Jews, assimilated professionals, who already subscribed to the *New Yorker* and donated to museums, were fiercely opposed to the influx of these peasants. Who could blame them?

My grandparents were unprepared for urban environments. These people had post-traumatic stress syndrome, and they'd had it for two thousand years. They passed it on. It's the Jewish version of an heirloom. Neurosis is an art form. You give it to your children, and it's indelible. Forget land or stock. Who needs jewelry or property? Some drunken barbarian will just steal it. Take these psychic deformations instead. Believe me, once you've got hypochondria, anxiety, manic depression, terror, insomnia, multiple personalities, rage, obsessive-compulsive disorders, and hallucinations, you've got something permanent.

"Always prepare for the worst," my grandmother, we'll call her Esther, would say. "That way, you'll never be disappointed. And you think this is bad. Wait. Worse is coming."

My group was profoundly ignorant. These people hadn't mastered addition or subtraction. Quantum mechanics and the subconscious? My people didn't even know where the Danube was. Those Chagall paintings of Jewish villages, men with beards and blue violins? Snow enameling domed churches? The woman on a bridge with a hat and rouged lips, her mouth promising to taste of onions and blueberries? You know the canvases I mean. White horses on fields like ornaments? The rustic table with a flowered cloth and a glazed bowl containing two bananas like mated canaries? Spasms of rain falling like an inverted ocean on the sable-haired young wife? The one who looks like she's planning to change her name to Katrina, drink absinth, be unfaithful, read smuggled novels in French, and run away to Vienna? And the lovers holding hands, floating between spires? Well, Chagall left my people out of his paintings.

You know artists. They're sensitive. They revise.

They edit. My relatives didn't know physics or anatomy. They knew the ground was hard and finding a ditch with a turnip in it was a party.

My people were the ones hanging the goat upside down the bloody wooden bucket. Chagall painted the goat instead of them. My grandparents were in the hovel, eating month-old borscht, air stained from nicotine, urine, and kerosene. Or maybe they didn't stay in the village long enough for Chagall to paint. They were lurching between cataclysms. The barber said they soiled his scissors with lice. The baker wouldn't give them credit. Even the rabbi wouldn't visit. He claimed he had priorities and they gave him migraines. They couldn't learn geometry, how to swim, or stop at red lights. When the shack burned down, they sat in a ravine for years like chained dogs.

They couldn't even invent a past with a single exception to impoverishment. I used to ask, "Do we have anyone of distinction in our family? A rabbi? A doctor? A learned man or woman anywhere in our family tree?" No. "How about a guy who owned a store with leather goods? He sold shoes and boots, maybe?" No. Just centuries of people with genetic trauma, curled up in rocky crevices of the Carpathian Mountains, waiting to get raped, looted, hung, drawn and quartered, imprisoned, conscripted, and tortured. I'll tell you how poor these people were. They thought a candle and a potato was a good time.

It wasn't a family tree. It was a thornbush. I'd ask

if there were there any happy memories? Happy and memory were like solving the theory of force fields. They weren't concepts that could fit in the same equation. Call them pre-Holocaust survivors. They'd spent two thousand years in their own version of gulags and concentration camps. They just managed to drift off before the official roundup and cattle-car call to Auschwitz and Dachau. They walked or hitched cart rides to the ships in Western Europe. I think this was the Russian version of what Castro did at Mariel. Steerage wasn't just brimming with intelligent, energetic individuals motivated by a spiritual connection to God and the SAT. There were irrevocably psychologically tarnished people in those storage containers. Lunatics. Sociopaths. Alcoholics. People with the genetic wiring for criminal activities, drug addiction, gambling, and excess. They had never seen a book or toilet. But they possessed a propensity for flexibility with the rules, the consensual interpretations.

Eventually, they found a place to sleep and cook cabbage and borscht. It took a generation. When they were convinced the Cossacks and Nazis weren't coming immediately, they began to relax and enjoy themselves. They even thought in terms of recreation.

In our family, cigarettes were a hobby. Surviving long enough to get lung cancer was an achievement. Heart attacks were our other recreational activity. Of course, that's a more skilled endeavor. Lung cancer, you know what to do. You just keep buying cartons of Lucky Strikes and matches, and you engage in continual acts of flame and breath and nicotine. It's what we call Jewish yoga.

But heart attacks require more dedication and behavioral discipline. Constant training and sacrifice. We considered it more a sport than a mere hobby. It was the next step up.

My brother, Sid, your uncle Sid, was our prototype heart-attack seeker. You need to recognize you have a calling. You must have the skill and the will. Heart attacks are like the Jewish triathlon. It took four to actually kill him. You can't just get that enormous final seizure from anxiety. You must relentlessly contribute to your condition. Keep your weight up, remain sedentary, and avoid contact with doctors.

Sid was 270 lbs. of cholesterol, alcohol, and nicotine. He never lifted anything heavier than a ladle. He only moved when it was absolutely necessary, like if he was down to his final carton of cigarettes, last bottle of vodka, and only had a few pounds of butter and cream cheese left. Only then would he rise from the sofa and drive to a market.

Heart attacks have rules. It's not a mystery. You maintain your obesity and cholesterol. When you get the first warning signs, like chest pain and borderline diabetes, you're making progress. You celebrate with latkes in sour cream. You feel encouraged. Then you raise your alcohol and calorie intake. You have a goal now, in sight. Full-on diabetes. None of that baby borderline crap. Diabetes is like completing the half-mile in a marathon.

You stay in training by stocking cabinets with cigarette cartons and vodka gallons. You buy a new TV with a dozen remote-control devices. Sure it costs, but you look at it as an investment. Strategic planning. You must remain sedentary. It's a good feeling, comfortable and reassuring to know you've got a remote control in your bathrobe pocket, on the sofa, coffee table, TV set, and in the cigarette carton and vodka stashes. And they're not just in kitchen cabinets. They're hidden under pillows and inside lamps, tucked into jackets in back closets. You know the drill. You treat the stuff with the cunning of a smack junky.

You learn the tricks. It's good to stay in your bathrobe. But it has to have multiple pockets. Uncle Sid kept two packs of cigarettes and a few lighters attached to his body at all times. It's also soothing to wear a bathrobe as a ritual garment. It helps you remember you're already dressed for the paramedics and ambulance. It validates your sense of being sick and becoming worse. Stay in character long enough and everybody recognizes you're an invalid.

One time I went on a car trip with my brother. It was an emergency. His wife had left him. She took everything over a weekend. Sid comes back from Vegas and the house is empty. You must have heard.

That problem when he got disbarred, the irregularities with his bookkeeping and the IRS. He did a little time. It happens. He was always sloppy. Anyway, his kids won't take his collect calls. I know it's a crisis when he telephones me.

This was a big deal. Sid did not wear clothing. Just an overcoat on top of his permanent bathrobe. But he had to locate his car keys and wallet. Then a full-service gas station because my brother avoiding moving. If somebody else can bend over for you, let them. It costs more, but sometimes a few dollars must be spent in pursuit of your passion. We drove to an Indian reservation where they fill up the trunk with untaxed cigarette cartons. They load the cardboard boxes directly in. Just takes a credit card.

Still, levels of psychological preparation are required. It's like getting in the zone in sports. You must sustain constant levels of massive fear. Anxiety is the secret Jewish fuel. My brother Sid was unswerving in his quest for sudden death. He had a few drunk car accidents on his way to nicotine and pastry dispensaries. After the last crash, he got a limp and needed a cane. Of course, real discernible physical injury is the Jewish version of a Purple Heart. No one can argue that you don't need to be in your bathrobe on the sofa after that. You have the cane to prove it. My brother got his first heart attack at forty-one. It was a good try, but not definitive.

If you could have seen his disappointment. His

pain was unbearable. He'd have to try harder. They gave him medications. Prozac on general principle. But that happens to everyone in our family. By the time we tell a doctor our name and impressionistically describe our condition, including our interpretation of the symptoms, the guy has his prescription pad out. And he's made a note in big black letters at the top of the chart that says MAJOR PSYCHIATRIC DISTURBANCES. Then pills for hypertension. Insulin for the diabetes. Anti-inflammatories. Antidepressants. "They're trying to poison me," Sid would say. He flushed that stuff down the toilet.

Our people are still amazed to have indoor plumbing. They flaunt it. They can't help themselves. They're always talking about flushing things down the toilet. Wherever they live, they immediately remodel the bathroom and build a backup. Some people collect stamps, rare editions, stocks, antiques. Our relatives accumulate bathrooms.

Finally, Sid got Valium and Seconal. This he took. He mixed it with vodka. That's the Jewish version of a nighttime snack. White Russians with Seconal, a pound of pastrami, a brick of cheese, and a rye bread to stick it in. Impaling cold cuts into baked goods is another version of Jewish sex. But you have to hand it to Sid. He kept trying. He didn't get the definitive claw in his chest, the strike three and you're out until he was fifty-three. By then, we'd forgotten he was still technically alive.

Of course, his funeral was cutting-edge minimal. We have a tradition of leaving the infirm behind. You can't keep up with the oxcart? So long, Mom. We'll send you a postcard from America. Just stay right here. It's a nice ditch. See, it's got a bush. It's scenic. Or maybe you can hobble back to the village. See if Sis with the cough we left behind with her bucket to spit blood in is still around. Or the baby with the leaking eye we knew we'd never get through customs. Or maybe Max who cut his arm off with an ax last winter. He's probably still there. We'll send you all tickets over later. Tragic? It was a victory. Sid knew the rules. He had perseverance and never deviated from his goal. Who says you can't beat the house?

You feel that lucky, kid? Think you can just walk out the door into another life? You're a big girl now. Place your bet. Go try to beat the house. And don't forget, I warned you.

Transmission to Los Angeles
#1

*M*Y FAMILY DECIDED TO LEAVE LOS Angeles in a period after the riots and last major earthquake, which shook us more than psychologically. The glass in our windows splintered, we were cut. Los Angeles had finally spilled our blood. We held each other as aftershocks rolled through and under us like waves on a ship lost at sea. It was days without electricity or water. Car alarms and sirens provided the grotesque sound track. Streets were chaotic with people driving and walking without destinations, circular, predatory, and frightened. You could see what they were thinking by their erratic movements and feral exhausted eyes. One more night without water and lamps, and we'll be barbarians again, sharpening sticks and beating our neighbors for the last Evian and crackers.

If the quake had been a single increment higher, our apartment would have collapsed. It was as if the physical world was finally reflecting our interior fragility. Within we were shoddy, barely glued in place, lacking sufficient insulation, and close to breaking apart ourselves. The increasingly combat-zone quality of life, the stresses and obligations of raising a family in Los Angeles had accumulated and were forming a distinct morphology. It was a nightmare you couldn't wake up from.

There were equations we couldn't resolve. A significant factor in relocating was our inability to afford a home in a neighborhood where we wanted to live. Just a quiet pocket, a protected insinuation of green, where we didn't need to install bars on the windows, wear bulletproof vests, and carry concealed weapons.

We found the opportunity to move when my husband joined the faculty of a small private college in the Allegheny Mountains of remote rural western New York State. I looked at a dozen houses in a single afternoon and bought the last one I saw. I was struck by its unique charm. I thought, "It's the ultimate Topanga Canyon or Marin County house at one-tenth the price."

That was one afternoon in May. I suspected there were problems. It was a 150-year-old farmhouse surrounded by a ring of 60 apple trees, some old and wild, all blossoming white and singular, simultaneously starched and fragile. A house on a hill, secluded inside nearly 100 acres beyond which there were only maple, oak, birch, and pine forest for hundreds of miles.

The house would have to be updated, I knew that. It must be made more conventionally Los Angeles, urban, modern, sophisticated, and private. It would have to be painted. The walls must be white, of course, and new fixtures installed. Still, I sensed there was something wrong with the essential layout. I would wake up in the throes of doubt in the middle of car alarm–and ambulance siren–saturated nights. Was it a mistake? By August, as we drove across the country, I had forgotten what the house actually looked like. Somewhere in the heartland, certainly by Indiana, I was convinced I had purchased a decrepit, wind-throttled barn.

In truth, the house is sturdy gray hemlock and flagstone. During our first winter, which was the coldest in years, nothing leaked, broke, or collapsed. The interior is a sequence of woods, floors and walls, ceilings with beams from abandoned railway ties and planks from barns. There are unexpected steps, angles and windows everywhere. I spent months staggering from the brilliance of the landscape, how the view from each glass pane is different. That summer, I watched deer three feet from where I stood, memorizing the orchard turning yellow then red, while fields of sweet corn went to straw.

Fall was a siege of inflamed maples, leaves like wine and fire. They are not burgundy or magenta, but more intense then anything I have words for. I understand harvest rituals for the first time; the shapes and colors of Halloween that were contrived and surreal in urban Los Angeles, remote, incomprehensible vestiges from another culture suddenly resonate. Here, seasons form a natural progression of events. The earth announces what time it is. When maple leaves are the orange of actual pumpkins, there's a clarification. It's like solving an equation. And we have real bats. We had one trapped in the house for a week. We observed him flying through our sunroom through the glass, hideous, like a rat with wings. We now immediately shut our doors, always.

Still, there was the gnawing problem with the house interior. The upstairs has three bedrooms and a large bathroom with an enormous claw-footed tub, and a recently installed pine sauna. I planned to add another bathroom to the master bedroom. Then I was informed that the roof couldn't be altered. The roof is this house's Pandora's box. It's inviolate.

It had not occurred to me that our family of three would share a bathroom. I would not have purchased this house if I suspected that. I suppose that's where it began, the shift in my thinking. It started with the upstairs bathroom and communicating directly with our teenager. "You bathe first. Then it's my turn." Once you are using a bathroom with your spouse and adolescent, the phenomenon of being a one-telephone, one-computer, one-television family becomes increasingly plausible. When the difficulty and expense of adding equipment and finding reliable workmen is a fact of life, the idea of being a family that shares possessions and space becomes increasingly tolerable.

In Los Angeles, we had separate bathrooms, of course, our own phone lines, computers, electronic devices, and audio systems. This was a given. We had our adult life, and our teenager had her version of events. In fact, our more affluent friends had separate wings of their houses, parent-versus-child areas, as befits people who inhabit the same structure but have completely different activities, friends, vocabularies, and diversions. We manifest our impulses and necessities in our architecture. There are profound philosophical implications within design decisions.

Privacy between family members is a basic law of the urban order. It's in the bones of the houses themselves, a fundamental structural imperative. Decoded, it says to your child, "You and your problems, incipient vices, confusions, communiqués with the outside, which we do not monitor or even want to know about, take them to your room, now. We give you things, and in return, we expect you to be compliant and absent."

The intrinsic allure of this 150-year-old farmhouse I impulsively embraced is embedded in the wood itself, in the view of the valley and ponds, which I can see now that the leaves have fallen. The appeal of this house is that it can't be conventionalized or made more like Los Angeles, not unless we gut and rebuild it. The charm of this house is that it is, irrefutably, in every angle and grain in each plank of oak and maple, a family home.

I had not considered the psychology of architecture in quite this way, how intensely the arrangement of rooms in houses reflects and manifests our roles, the tangible shapes of our affections, the quality of our intimacy, and the value of interaction versus its absence. I hadn't considered the level of mutual tolerance and cooperation living together necessitates.

The texture of tangibly interwoven lives is like a fine fabric, muslin, perhaps, and certain hand-stitched cottons that are washed throughout a lifetime and become not unlike silk. This process implies hands. Our farmhouse was built in 1849 by people who expected it to stand for hundreds of winters. They planned to spend their decades, their meals and bathing facilities, their entertainments, thoughts, anxieties, inspirations and visitors together. Personal behaviors and external events were entwined. They accommodated the unsanitized versions of their interactions as an intrinsic process.

In retrospect, although we believed we had our own interpretation of the family values culturally extolled in a manner more stringent than fashion, we were actually superficial in our involvement. We thought we were participating appropriately, checking homework, enforcing bed by nine, personal hygiene supervision, frequent teacher conferences, dinner together on a semiregular basis with an obligatory but keep-it-short daily synopsis. We were satisfied with sound bites. But compared with the physical and emotional choreography we have now, it's obvious that in Los Angeles we merely inhabited the same building while engaging in mutually exclusive pursuits. Perhaps that's why it felt like an obligation. It was like a second job.

There's a family room in this house with a television, fireplace, and record player, and the three of us are here much of the time. The kitchen is central, all rooms lead to and from it. Cooking and what it implies, survival and nurturing, are not abstractions that occur offstage. The kitchen is rarely seen in the ideal houses of Los Angeles, the ones we wish we could purchase. Kitchens are like bathrooms, specifically designed to be private. Kitchens are where the live-in works. Such rooms are not part of the entertaining portions of homes, but camouflaged and removed from sight. They're like the house's covert cul-de-sac you don't want to know about.

Here the kitchen is immediately visible. You see it, exposed, from the front doorway and living room. The activities that occur there are prominent and unconcealed. My daughter and I have both learned to cook since we moved here, to a town without takeout. We have discovered recipes and how to decipher them. Together, we picked apples, transported them in baskets, peeled and boiled them, making applesauce we put in jars on shelves in the larder. Vacuum sealing was a process I did not anticipate encountering in this incarnation or any other. But we vacuum-sealed our apples as a family adventure, my husband boiling the glass jars. He's a biochemist and feels competent in this capacity.

It snows, we eat September applesauce, and it occurs to me that family experience is not a two-week vacation. Perhaps it's something you pick from tree limbs, carry in wicker baskets, boil in pots, and eat four months later while winds howl.

We haven't purchased a new computer. We don't use the one we have much anymore. In Los Angeles, where our friends were an hour and a half of hard traffic away, it was easier to communicate in cyberspace. They might as well have been in Michigan or Madagascar. No one in this family is online much anymore. We are not stationed at the screen, with pseudonyms and assorted transitory fictional identities. We pass our frozen pond embroidered by deer and bear and rabbit tracks, and the ground is telling us a story. At some point during this year of transition, we divested ourselves of virtual reality and walked out into a real and bitterly freezing world. When it's this cold, the subtext becomes less important. There is nothing ambiguous about seventeen below zero.

We didn't get extra phone lines, either. We began to know who was calling and why, what occasions punctuate their lives and how they affect us. Of course, we have extensions in our bedrooms, but it's surprising how little we use them. I know our fourteen-year-old daughter is thinking on a level of intricacy and detail I could not have imagined possible or even considered desirable in Los Angeles.

I was beguiled by this house for subliminal associations I am just recognizing. There's an elaborate subconscious architecture here. Perhaps I sensed that a family is an organic symbiotic unit inhabiting the same physical structure in real time. It is not distinct existences stuck like bad skin grafts in an illusion of common facilities. When you have separate wings in your house, individual schedules, activities, amusements, and commitments, family values is just another sound bite.

We are two country miles from the college, one winding road without a traffic light. My husband comes home for lunch. Or we meet in town. I go to psychology, science, and art lectures at the university. I attend openings at the school gallery and campus musical and theatrical performances. I'm taking classes at the college, drawing with charcoal, and considering ceramics, how clay might feel in my fingers. What if I arranged flowers I had planted as bulbs in vases I constructed with my hands? Would that be a kind of poem in three dimensions?

I'm learning to identify birds and bake pies. I'm also beginning to recognize the moods of my adolescent, how to read her face, which is a pendulum across a fast-forward epic. Sometimes we drink coffee together in the afternoons and I stay current, know who she eats lunch with, can name her favorite band that particular week, and which of her class-mates has fallen from her favor. I ask. I pause and listen. Sometimes I hear. I understand silence, too, is a distinct punctuation and terrain. We listen to music. We take turns selecting records. We read po-etry and novels out loud in front of the fireplace. We argue. We laugh. We debate. We're not resorting to charades for entertainment yet, but we are verbally engaged.

I didn't have the energy for that in Los Angeles, where I spent inordinate amounts of time anguish-ing over my career and its monumental importance to my family, region, and epoch. I also squandered excessive amounts of time considering the intrica-cies of people I didn't know or even want to know. When I took my emotional pulse, I discovered I was thinking about Courtney Love, Michael Stipe, Bob Dylan, or Brad Pitt. I was infiltrated and colonized by images and media, the way the fissures of alleys in Los Angeles are networks embossed with layers of graffiti. It was in the air and it was in me. My windows offered an unyielding expanse of abraded stucco. I practiced not seeing. My teenager was intrusive and inconvenient, so I encouraged her to be inconspicu-ous and distant. We spoke in passing, in fragments. We might as well have been grunting.

I am often asked here, in the Allegheny Mountains, if I'm experiencing culture shock. Is this isolated rural enclave seven hours from Boston an overwhelming change? I say no. Los Angeles was the shock, the constant translation and adjustment. This is the house of my dreams. In this town, it is possible they speak a dialect in which I may be fluent. That's not a crucial element. If you knew my family, you'd understand why people have been, for me, an acquired taste. But this is a landscape I could fall in love with. But then again, falling in love with landscapes is what L.A. women do. It doesn't necessarily imply betrothal or marriage.

Transmission to Los Angeles
2

$\mathcal{I}$T'S OUR SECOND AUTUMN IN THE Allegheny Mountains, and this year I know what the changing leaves signify. I have a vocabulary and reference points with this region now, experience and systems of measurement. First the sounds like an ocean just behind the trees, a stark gray rushing howl. I know what winter is, and I'm terrified.

Last fall, I was simply astonished. Maples and oaks turned in a series I didn't have a palette for. Ambers, russets, and oranges that initiated me into the Halloween ritual of pumpkins for the first time. It was an induction. Halloween had been merely another abstract consumer occasion in Los Angeles. What could the absurd vestiges of harvest festivals have to do with us?

These maples are not the California curry and inflammation, not the disruptive calligraphy of errant neon, but a further yellow, subtle and refined. It must be the basis for prayer, ceremonies of purity and redemption, why there are lighthouses and candles. Then leaves the reds of dissidence and insurrection.

I think of danger, seduction and elegance, cycles and completion. I saw the forest as a girl from the mock-tropics of Los Angeles and was dazzled,

So this is the European-ordained version of shedding and release. Maples and oaks were a chronology of burgundies, wines, brandies, and clarets. Clearly, a forest for alcoholics. I considered the importance of intoxication through fermented beverages, a significant recurring motif since before *Beowulf.* This was a further layer being imparted by currents of wind.

I was on my knees, feverishly stuffing daffodil, iris, tulip, hyacinth, and lily bulbs into the cool moist earth. This was a triumph unto itself. If you are from city slums, you only encounter the earth if you fall down or happen to be searching for objects you c in exchange for dimes and quarters, barter, or take to a pawnshop. The unsanctioned of urban centers do not voluntarily touch the ground. They even try to take their stab and bullet wounds standing.

I had a dozen burlap sacks containing one hundred bulbs in each. I was planting the perimeter of the house. I had standard flower beds, experimental and control areas, and the completely haphazard approach of randomly dropping a bulb into a hole wherever I happened to be.

Why was I gardening like this? I'm from Los Angeles. I'm wildly excessive. I do everything in bursts of frenzy, as much and fast as possible, and then I get serious and crank it up a notch. Where I come from, this is not perceived as manic, but necessary and normal.

I was on my knees near our house, surrounded by burlap bags, and my assorted digging implements, trowels, shears, and baskets, when a stranger stopped his car and approached me. He introduced himself as a local hunter. He had permission to shoot the deer on the acres adjacent to our property. He'd been hunting here for years, and had I seen any deer around?

"There are four deer here. Two doe and two yearlings. But I'm extremely fond of them," I explained. "I consider them *my* deer." I looked up into his eyes, the way we do in Los Angeles, when we say something is *ours*.

"Then you better take a picture of them," the hunter replied.

I was stung. I took rolls of photographs of deer grazing among the sixty apple trees surrounding our house. I imagined enclosing our deer to protect them. I could lure them into the garage, lock them inside, and feed them what? Fantastic salads? That's something a Los Angeles woman, even in remote rural exile, could handle. A wheelbarrow piled with varieties of lettuce, carrots, tomatoes, and perhaps a bit of cabbage for accent. I envisioned trudging through snow with my wheelbarrow to four agitated, captured, and angry animals. It would be good exercise, but was it plausible?

"Have you been in winter before?" a neighbor inquired.

I listed my snow exposures, which included weekends in Aspen, Vail, Lake Tahoe, Banff, Squaw Valley, Big Bear, Mammoth, and Santa Fe. And I'd once given a reading commemorating the opening of a library in Juneau.

"But have you *lived* in the North?" my neighbor wanted to know.

"Oh, yes. I lived in Berkeley for seven years," I assured her.

Then winter came. Visually, the forests, hills, and valley looked like a punitive fringe of Russia in a harsh winter in a severe century. Last December, in a cameo performance, the sun came out precisely three times. January was rarely above five degrees. It snowed on Easter. It snowed on Mother's Day. Berkeley was not adequate preparation for this.

Of course, the people who have spent twenty and thirty years in our rural enclave numbering two thousand, in the foothills of the Allegheny Mountains just a breath above Pennsylvania, wanted to see how a family from Los Angeles would conduct themselves during this dramatic geographic and climatic revision. It's not that they've been withholding their affections, precisely, but our behavior has been closely observed.

Would we complain at dinner parties about the brutal and relentless winter, contract cabin fever, make derogatory comments about the lack of external stimulation? After the romance of trees swaying in spectrums of almond and cinnamon, after the glamour of maple leaves dropping like red flares, would we react as typical urbanites? Run off to Miami or Aruba as often as possible? Would we make it through the year? Would we stay?

The truth is, we've managed. If you can live in Los Angeles, you can survive anywhere. We are experts in extremities, unreasonable forces, and cruelly inexplicable seizures of the elements. There are harsh atmospheres you ascertain on temperature charts, and the more complex corridors of extravagant immoderation that are measured by the human heart. We are well versed in savage intensities, we who have called Los Angeles home.

Yes, we've been snowed in here in our Allegheny village. But there were periods when we couldn't leave our apartment in Los Angeles, either. I remember standing on my roof during the riots of the early 1990s, looking east across a city so dense with burning buildings and smoke that the horizon was a fence of grays, planes couldn't land, and I wondered how my husband would drive home from Downtown. It required the strategy of a combat mission and took nine hours.

I once attended a luncheon during a sudden Topanga Canyon wildfire. First one guest and then another would be summoned to the phone, instructed to come home immediately and evacuate. Some were informed they had half an hour to pack a lifetime into suitcases and cardboard boxes. Or else they were told to find a hotel; their house was already gone, burned to the ground.

"Doesn't the isolation bother you?" another neighbor asks.

Apparently, our new community envisions Southern California through a veil of airbrushed images, vividly distorted juxtapositions lacking context. They believe one walks out the door into a postcard. They assume everything is a short drive on the Pacific Coast Highway. They don't calculate road closures, mud- and rockslides, floods, fires, or traffic. The ocean is a four-hour drive, an excursion in tedium. It's easier to fly to Hawaii.

They believe the 3″ × 5″ laminated version of Los Angeles exists, the official stylized images of motion pictures and T-shirts. Cameras don't lie. Los Angeles is cerulean currents, as if carried by clouds from mesas. Monsoons with lightning in fierce electric neon spasms deposit their rains in Santa Monica Bay. In such imaginary skies, one watches stars reveal their complicated celestial choreography, their metallic orbits echoing in transit like modulated chimes.

They don't know the air is rancid; avenues are stitched with neglected tenements, windows and doors webbed with metal grates. You cage yourself in for protection. Los Angeles is a theoretical inlet now, an artifact of what never was. When movies are filmed along that coast now, the cast and crew need antibiotics and avoid contact with the fluids.

No, we're not bothered by the enforced isolation of this seven-month arctic winter. In Los Angeles, we often elected to stay home simply because we couldn't face two hours of voluntary carcinogenic chemical exposure and freeway hazards in an attempt to arrive at a landscape resembling a postcard of some other beach town in another era. We'd had our fill of sun striking asphalt with the force of a 9-mm semi-automatic ricocheting off walls in waves like tiny flames. Afternoons of conflagrations and firestorms. That was the workweek. Weekends were dedicated to repairing ourselves, the recuperation required to begin the ordeal again.

"But you must miss your friends," our new acquaintances point out.

They don't realize our friends lived seventy or eighty miles away, in Costa Mesa or Santa Barbara, La Jolla or Thousand Oaks. They were like virtual friends we rarely saw. We had conflicting schedules, deadline overwork, and the furious juggling of providing children with music lessons, sporting events, orthodontists, tennis lessons and cultural activities, all of which we had to drive them to and from. It was more an exercise in stamina than a celebration of the classics. Everyone was sullen.

Our neighbors don't know about the Los Angeles rite of the playdate. The meetings between children that necessitate special scheduling. And they don't play. They have nanny-supervised auditions. If one gets a callback, one might be short-listed as a potential acquaintance. If one performed beyond all expectation, a sort of probationary partial friendship might ensue.

"But you had the theater. The orchestra," a potential friend notes.

Her tone implies our evenings were a sequence of European ballets, New York cast theater productions, and arias presented by legends. Of course, we had to navigate miles of combat zone to arrive at such renowned entertainments. We had to literally step over the homeless, cutting a wide berth around men and women who had lost their minds, who slump on sidewalks, loiter in parking lots, their exposed skin the unique uniform charcoal of big city filth. They eat from trash cans and sleep in thorny foliage beneath freeways. A legion of the discarded, shivering, cursing invented deities and long-buried relatives. Did encounters like that interfere with our pursuit of cultural events? Was that worse than three hours of blizzard highway? I can fill in the blank to that question. The answer is yes.

In truth, the fact that art is now a pilgrimage is stunning and humbling. In good weather, it's an hour and a half drive to a movie theater. A museum is a full-day drive. It renders the event what it should be, namely, an experience. Seeing an exhibit in Buffalo, three hours of icy rolling hills away, I thought, yes, this is precisely what art should be, the revelation at the end of a journey. And the exhibition or performance should be received reverentially. Hazardous travel is a requirement. You must pay for this dangerous expedition with your time. It should inform the entire discussion on the drive home. In other words, it should be profoundly important.

Art has traditionally been displayed in settings and under circumstances meant to be defining. Once one risked bandits and pirates, kidnapping and unusual bacteria to see a canvas or statue. Art wasn't intended to be filler between social events. This is one method by which art has been degraded in our current national configuration.

"What about all the recreation?" another acquaintance inquires.

They must be envisioning an amalgam of memorized footage. Los Angeles is sailing the coast north, bike paths curving gracefully across exotically floral-laden bluffs along the lip of sapphire coves, hiking trails branching off to canyons of eucalyptus and pine. Actually, there is scant recreation in Los Angeles. During our final incoherent year there, we joined a sailing club. With the exception of summer Sundays, we often didn't see another boat all day. Anyone who can afford a boat is too busy to use it.

Or perhaps they only sail in waters considered more chic and prestigious.

I want to explain to our town folk that there is no genuine play in Los Angeles. Everyone is preoccupied, overburdened, doing more than they can, and it's not nearly enough. Recreation is for vacations in Hawaii, the Riviera, and Tahiti. Typically, people engage in manifestly arrogant exercise regimes for weight control and body appearance. It has nothing to do with pleasure or scenery. It's a form of peer pressure–induced elective torture. Do joggers on the paths and sides of boulevards in cities look like they're enjoying themselves? But that's just a warm-up. Wait until their personal trainers arrive, equipped with the latest six-week routine.

Now I'm planting tulips in a delirium again. We survived our first year and as I dig in the earth, I remember the startling bulbs emerging after winter, tiny triangular peaks resembling jade and pink teeth rising tentatively from the slow-motion melting ice, beds of infants with just-opening mouths.

What did I do during this first year? What alternative avenues did I invent to amuse myself? I enrolled in classes at the university, printmaking, photo-lithography, and collage. I attended ecology seminars and molecular biology lectures. I listened to music, actually sat down and read the lyrics I always said I would, some time, if I had the time. I surveyed our property, noting where a garden had once been, how deer carve paths through grasses to the creeks, bent grasses showing where they sleep. Then I walked down our dirt road, gradually building my stamina, one farm with corn or sheep, potatoes or chickens, at a time. It's not my usual competitive walking, either. I don't imagine I'm being timed. I'm not compelled to find and cross a finish line.

I discovered a small aptitude for cooking. I had to reread recipes dozens of times. They seemed to be written in another language I was unfamiliar with, the lingo of cooking and all it implies. Drain. Sieve. Mash. Braise. Knead. Puree. There was an abundance of ambiguity. Where does one draw the line between flaking and sprinkling, grating, slicing, mincing and dicing? How slow is moderate stirring? Am I genetically equipped for defatting and desalting? And the measurements, the yields and equivalents seemed insurmountable and produced math anxiety. Pounds, ounces, cups, tablespoons and their divisions, not to mention the contingencies of hot and soft, cooked and uncooked, raw or powdered, evaporated or fresh. Once, I baked seventy consecutive pies to feel the dough without trembling, and successfully roll it out and place it in a pie tin.

I engaged in an active correspondence necessitating pens and the postal service. My husband and I chopped wood, painted walls, tiled floors, repaired fences. We've discovered we didn't need sadistic and carefully scheduled fitness programs, after all.

Maintaining a 150-year-old house with 4 now mowed and planted acres is providing substantial exercise for a middle-age couple. We haven't gained a pound.

If you are intrinsically self-contained, it doesn't matter where you are but rather what you are. The story isn't better on Main Street, Santa Monica than Main Street in Allegheny. The story is in the quality of the narrative you bring to it, with you, the sophistication, clarity, and synthesis you devise.

Incidentally, I did not see that hunter again. Our four deer returned in late summer. I see them at sundown, crossing the orchard, eating their way toward our house. There are five now, and they're the size of mules. In the forest beyond, maples are the color of sunflowers and silk scarves. I walk often, knowing snow will soon make that impossible. Oddly, I'm living more in the moment than ever, confiscating a patch of sunlight to pull weeds before rain, letting clouds define my hours and activities, sensing I'm more flexible than I thought. And I suspect our neighbors are beginning to believe we may actually stay.

Let them presume what they want. We're from Los Angeles. We take it as it comes. And we take it as it goes. When you come from the illusionary oasis at the end of the other farther coast, permanent encampments seem unlikely. But we are here, now.

Transmission to Los Angeles
#3

$\mathscr{S}$OMETIMES THE RITES OF PASSAGE are simple and manifest, like the landmasses, islands, and peninsulas on nautical charts. We know currents and depths with astonishing precision. They're indisputable. Some afternoons are like emotional compass points. They tell us we have reached a distinct era in our erratic journey. Such junctures arrive with almost supernatural clarity, erased of complexity and ambivalence.

I felt this unassailable definition when I purchased my new address book. It was proof. A cumulative and unequivocal sequence propelled me to an unforeseen typography. I was no longer on an extended vacation or sabbatical. I contemplated my new address book, and in the contemporary matrix, rife with a multiplicity of simultaneously competing interpretations, I possessed that rare commodity. Certainty.

I held the address book and a black pen. I had, in fact, moved. It wasn't hallucinatory, and it wasn't temporary. We are now registered voters and official tax-paying residents of the State of New York. But an address book implies more. It's a confluence and terminal to confront identity and take stock. It's like spring-cleaning on a cellular level. It's a psychological autopsy. One doesn't simply transcribe existing entries onto fresh pages. There is a winnowing, an evaluation, editing and discarding.

I had gradually become someone else. Now I clearly saw the many who were impermeable, inscrutable sketches, problematic, unreliable or just business. There were the beautiful, witty and accomplished, prestigious adornments to one's social calendar, but we hadn't crossed the bridge to actual friendship and we never would. We had endured the sort of audition and short-listing our children do at playdates. But we had not progressed beyond the probationary stage. These were the first names I excised. They wouldn't be coming to my apple orchard, which is not a destination location, offers no four-star restaurants, or the possibility of encountering other celebrities on our hiking paths. There were no events for which they would need rare wardrobe accessories or embossed invitations. I recognized this and their zip codes were no longer relevant. The more haunting and resonant question is: Had they ever been?

Some entry possibilities were more than casual. They were, in fact, friends. There was a curious, disorienting moment when I realized the only threads binding me to another was time and its lewd wounds. Did an accumulation of similar bruises form an adequate basis for a relationship? Did sharing a metaphorical cell during a punitive, indeterminate sentence in the chrome ruins of Los Angeles constitute friendship? Yes, we knew afternoons strained through metal bars, oppression and despair, the verbal insult like a slap across the face engraving an imprint does not fade. Rather, the pattern of sting settles into the interior grain like rogue DNA, twisting within, producing nightmares and more elaborate deviant conditions requiring mental health professionals and medications.

But would she actually summon the motivation and resources to take a plane to an airport like Buffalo and want to wander deer paths and identify birds? Would my apple orchard and ponds, maple trees and pantry of applesauce in glass jars satisfy her? No. I was fixed into place, her designated cellmate in a past gulag. Had my private transmutations registered on her sonar? No. Then the question became one of nostalgia and its statute of limitation. And with a single pen line, a woman known since childhood disappeared. In truth, she had ceased to exist as a friend in the specific ways by which I now calculate and enter into covenants of conclusion. She was gone. She had been absent for decades.

Conversely, for an act of grace and inspiration, a person I will probably not meet or hear from again, in Juneau, Alaska, will remain in my address book at least through the next cut. I can't approximate when that revision will occur, although I instinctively know it will. The woman, call her Suzanne, had insisted during our one conversation over lunch at the edge of a glacier that I take a helicopter in, actually land and touch ice in the process of calving. When I hesitated, she arranged the expensive transportation and sat next to me. Suzanne claimed the range of blues in a calving field would be like a private tattoo, an intricate weaving to wear permanently engraved on the fibers of my inner skin. For this invisible ink, she remains with me.

A new address book is an astonishment, a piece of time gouged out from the continuum, geometric and tangible. It's where we establish the base camp for our developing personality. We elucidate and formalize our current frontiers, and see what's shifted in the restless, rapturous dark while we slept. Behaviors have accumulated and made their own shape, their unique and unmistakable morphology.

For instance, we were lied to, manipulated, not reciprocally invited (in all seasons, both casual and formal), and betrayed in petty ways that nonetheless defiled the air. Actions and omissions have their subtext. On certain midmornings, the subterranean hieroglyphics become headlines. We can say that specific gestures of selfishness and dismissal are unacceptable. We pronounce the perpetrators offenders and remove their names and phone prefixes.

It's a form of private excommunication, banishment and burial. It's an announcement and enactment of values and codes that reflect who we now see in our mirror. It's simultaneously a sort of spiritual experience and an examination of elemental psychological processes, ethics, perhaps, and the nature of loyalty and forgiveness. It's like planting a banner or flag on another continent or planet. Decisions of a philosophical magnitude occur. Sometimes a map and star chart, a journal, calculator, and photographs are necessary. And there's nothing simple about this mathematics of blood.

The people I was carrying into the future dwindled. I found the ability to draw a black ink line through a name, severing their destiny from mine, increasingly easy. I possessed a curiously celebratory sense of freedom. It was like Indian summer, walking in a sundress through dried sunflowers and cornhusks, listening to birds and sensing you've inexplicably become clairvoyant. The air is charmed above acres like cut crystal.

Then I began to notice who was left. Rather than families, a surprising number of my remaining names were women alone. And a significant number no longer resided in Los Angeles, though it was in the City of Angels that we had met and become friends.

A new address book is both a moral document and an indication of sociological phenomena. Where were these former Los Angeles women, why had they departed, and where they living?

I met Diana when I taught a writing workshop in Riverside. The Santa Anas were a liquid calligraphy, hills burning as if by a demented fluid red hand. Fire season in hills of dry weeds and grasses. I remember they had considered canceling the class. The air was charged beyond electric, as if the brush in flame was communicating, exposing the process of transformation from twig to fire to smoke. A poet might attempt to decipher such an extravagantly malignant manifestation.

Diana was writing poetry, studying Spanish, California Indian creation myths, and collecting animal bones and bird feathers. She didn't know why. Her fingers craved unusual objects. The pen was insufficient. Diana sensed she might be moving toward sculpture. Later, we drove back roads through the Baja, bartering for whalebones in tent and shack fishing villages on stretches of coast where there were no hotels and we slept on sand near the car. Still later, we sailed to Catalina, took a dinghy skimming across phosphorescent coves, the seafloor seething like a continent beneath my sunburned thighs, seemingly alive and preparing to speak through a vivid glittering mouth. I wanted to know what the seafloor was saying, benediction or blasphemy.

Then Gwen, who had recently moved into a nearby apartment and was barely an acquaintance. The doorbell startled me. Gwen had decided I needed snow for my February birthday. It was an ad hoc surprise party, car filled with immediately on-demand available acquaintances, balloons, and noisemaking party toys. Gwen drove to Santa Barbara, then inland, into mountains. I was amazed, watching snow fall through groves of orange trees and in the distance, another sound, also indigenous, like foghorns and wind. Cathedral bells from a hillside Spanish mission, announcing the official invitation to prayer. Who would not want to fall to their knees, there, in the barest mist with snow asserting itself as a lace veil between the fat, bright groves of oranges? It was an unexpected juxtaposition of citrus and ice you taste and never forget. I inscribed her name into my address book. Perhaps there will be another birthday, somewhere, sometime.

I consider Julia, starting her life over at forty-five, how extraordinary that seemed to me twenty years ago. Julia resigned from her law firm and the bar to paint in Santa Cruz. Her studio, with angular panels of skylights, was set beneath redwood trees on a rolling hill above the ocean. That day, the coast was a glassy violet, faceted and polished. Wind-shredded redwood flakes and bronzed needles lay on the ground like cargoes of spilled cinnamon, and the breeze smelled of mint and chalky medicinal eucalyptus.

Why not begin an entire other career at forty-five, discover a discrete geography within, a further kingdom demanding to be externalized? The idea, alien and heretical to me then, is increasingly alluring. Certainly there are random resurrections, inexplicable and continual, just as there are tumors, fires, and plague. We are struck down. We are raised. There is another competing logic, more elegant and intricate than science knows. But I let the sea breeze, redwoods and eucalyptus, take this thought. It would be twenty years before I reconsidered it.

We who have spent decades in Los Angeles possess a capacity and intuition for alternative systems of interpretation. Perhaps we have a greater ease with the transitory, and the conviction that personality itself is a series of inspired idiosyncratic provisional solutions. The landscape tells us. It's in the crumbling cliffs above Malibu. It's in the ocean and shore tango that isn't erosion but a form of seduction. The dance before consummation.

My address book is a compendium of disclosure and confession. Diana now resides on a mesa outside Taos in a house she built herself from straw bales and adobe. It took five years to complete. She erected her sculpture studio first and slept there two years on a cot. Gwen is now a few hours beyond Portland, Oregon, and Julia a short drive from Missoula, Montana. Together, they are my representative sample of women who recognized their solitary impulses and withstood the pressure to pretend otherwise. Some are lesbian or they're divorced, widowed, or inhabit regions resistant to categories and labels. Their children have gone to college, married, or moved away. Or they chose to not reproduce.

We share the unprecedented freedom to express ourselves outside patriarchal borders. The patriarchy has set the perimeters of human perception, scales and proportion, philosophy and art, and how it is received and evaluated since the first stone tool, no doubt a skull-crushing instrument, was flaked. The patriarchy established and maintained the hierarchies of thought and behavior so long, it seems a natural feature, like the Rocky Mountains or Pacific Ocean, that which has always been. But all geographies are subject to change. Earthquakes. Droughts. Ages of ice. Orbs that fall without warning from skies. And time, which speaks in canyons, gives and takes forests, savannas, glaciers, species, and oceans in its passing.

Until the recent aberration of the nuclear family, women existed within extended blood groups, tribes, villages, and ultimately cities. Technology has made it viable for females to function outside the increasingly dubious protection of urban areas. With the availability of the fax, cell phone, computer, and e-mail, the parameters aren't about physical survival anymore. They are psychological, matters of individual events, and the values we assign to circumstances. A woman can check electronic news reports and pile wood into a stove as well as a man. The issues aren't hatchet-wielding techniques but the more fragile realms of loneliness and solitude, of phenomena viewed, interpreted, remembered, and perhaps loved alone.

Los Angeles is the prototypical feminine city, with its relentless flagrant insistence on the tropical, its sun setting in a debauchery of magenta while petals spill across alleys like inland seas of soft fire. The landscape resists convenient classification. It's not a city where rules are written in stone. The regulations are inscribed in a pastel script, containing a sense of sea waves, unusual punctuations and dialects.

Nuestra Senora, La Reina, Queen of the Angels, has given us a fertile postmodern plateau inhabited by women bearing the names of ancient cities and flowers. Women who change their names as their identity expands, and their birth names can no longer explain or contain their imagination. They discard them as inadequate representations of who they are becoming. Birth names may become inhibiting artifacts. Some women wear transitional names taken from stones and herbs with reputed powers. Women with bottles of gin in their bathrobes, hanging frayed sheets on terraces in a grit of dusk, consider their options. Such women have faces like epics. You could take their photographs and extrapolate the journeys they have taken.

You can recognize women in the process of metamorphosis. Their eyes are like the last lighthouse on the final peninsula at the end of the world. They have lit votives in windows for the lost. They have tended the campfires. Now they burn with intelligence from within. It projects from their eyes like beacons, not for sailors at sea, but rather to illuminate the path they are making with their bare feet across cement and cactus.

It is not a rejection of Nuestra Senora, Our Lady of Tolerance and Bitter Citrus. The female city, she of salt air, and skies above deserts that are a triumphant blue, simultaneously a distillation and a statement of concise purpose, like a treaty or constitution. Such a sky looks alive, a cobalt-skinned lizard organic above the ocotillo and barrel cactus.

That my address book is largely comprised of women without traditional families or the occupations they began their careers with is not a negative reflection on Los Angeles. In fact, it's the opposite. Los Angeles, so exorbitantly experimental, with her end-of-the-trail rough-hewn pragmatism, fascination with originality, and uncompromising recognition of aesthetics as a primary character, has birthed unique females for a radically postmodern, post-urban arena. Our Lady of agave and mantillas lifted a skirt and released her millennial daughters.

After all, America is a chronicle of passages. The European immigrant Atlantic crossings. Manifest Destiny and the wagon trains. The migrations of foreclosed farmers during the upheavals of the Depression. The '50s and '60s of the Beats, sanctifying the road itself, rather than the destination. And the millions in denim, ponchos, and backpacks who followed their indications of an illuminated path. Now the migrations of approved intellectual achievers, who receive visas. Where once we said bring us your hungry and yearning, we now say give us your scientists and research specialists. But others come, continual, running from wars and tyranny. They are covert and rarely granted governmental documents.

Each generation endorses its hierarchies of necessity. When I turn the pages of my address book, I can tell you something about the L.A. Woman thirty-something years after Jim Morrison gave her a universal, mythic identity. It's more than three decades later, and the L.A. Woman is entering the twenty-first century unencumbered by the burden of unwanted children, rules, and thousands of generations that tell her where she can't live and what she dare not do. We vote no, we will not be chattel and bodies that breed, repair your fishing nets and spears, and censor the words from our mouths.

In her time, the L.A. Woman has been the Lady of the Canyon, both Laurel and Topanga. She's carpooled as a Valley housewife in Woodland Hills and Encino. She's had an artist's loft Downtown, in Echo Park and Pasadena. She's lived by the ocean in Venice when Beats read poetry with bongo drums, and has written her first poems on napkins in coffee houses, and first novel in a bungalow perched along the canals. She's lived in Laguna Beach and Santa Monica where she carted children and their infrastructure to soccer practices, swim meets and recitals, supervised homework, and practiced yoga. In between, something happened.

Now the L.A. Woman has moved on. She's built her own house. She's learning to ride and keep horses in mountain pastures. She's living by kerosene and teaching herself Chinese and calligraphy by candlelight and lantern. She's closing mortgages by fax then practicing Tai Chi by a tributary of the Colorado. This year, she might spend her birthday in Prague, Katmandu, or Bali.

I decode my address book. This is what it says. Los Angeles did not fail the L.A. Woman. Rather, it prepared her to respond to the ravishment of color and texture, the intoxication of fragrances, of night vines imported from Brazil and Africa opening infant white mouths above curbs and alleys. And somewhere along the line, she just graduated, turned forty-something, and realized that for the first time, cities are optional for females. My address book is a directory of women living alone, at extreme edges of the map, looking out at mountains, mesas, and rivers, knowing they're not afraid.

Thoughts pass like clouds and stray hawks. Absence can be a form of abuse or a revelation. It's simply a pause in punctuation, like a comma or scalpel.

Some women practice rituals of sagebrush, tumble-weed, save salts from the North, keep tin boxes of juniper seeds in their linen. Such objects make daisies like volatile canaries and produce window boxes of strawberries in November, when winter resurfaces like a bad dream. They are vigilant. Their perfume is creosote and cedar. They can fast for weeks.

I have seen these women become ruthless, lean, lone assassins purified by clarity. They are lunar and exposed, mutinous, nervous and erratic. They have deliberately chosen this and rarely sleep. The sky is greasy with residues a promiscuous moon left. They prefer landscapes so literal, they're both acts of intimacy and a reprimand.

I know these women practice silence while deserts graze their backs, convinced there is love in every plaza in the gullies of saguaro and happenstance. They create their own prayers. Holy is the arroyo, the coyote, and cactus. Holy the bandits, the winds of sand like random bullets. Holy the tiny bruja rinsed by rain.

These are the women I may never speak to or see again. They live in my address book in pen. As to my new acquaintances, who all have the same prefix and practice identical prescribed postures of celebration and supplication, I've put their four digits in pencil.

Transmission to Los Angeles #4

*I*T'S BEEN MORE THAN THREE YEARS since I left the city of my birth. Only a native daughter, a woman who calls Los Angeles her hometown, could offer this confession.

I was raised in Los Angeles, married and divorced there more than once. There, I buried my father, mother, and recently, my younger brother. I gave birth to my daughter there. You do the math. It's a city of subtraction and ash.

In between, in Venice and Silverlake, Westwood, West Hollywood, and Beverly Hills, I wrote twelve books. I stood on decades of late afternoon balconies, watching sun set in oranges brutally metallic and chiseled with inhuman translucence. I thought my face would be scarred. And it was. Some psychological wounds are defining components the way external elements are, how wind weathers skin and sun tightens flesh like cured leather.

In the conceptual latitudes, museum pieces can't be excavated and displayed. One must struggle to retain the intangible elements of personal chronology before the sea breeze shreds them as it does bamboo and fronds.

The Los Angeles of my recreated childhood was a flat plain I knew with my legs and bare feet. I was intimate with canna-studded shortcut alleys, zigzagging between cement and hibiscus to the beach. The blue bus line of Pico Boulevard was my perimeter. It was the vein, the artery. My limits were as far as I could walk north along the coast and east to the La Cienega Tar Pits, where even the dinosaurs had somehow been trapped.

There were whispers of tattooed sailors in a port called San Pedro. I envisioned rum-ridden men with dragons inked on their arms emerging from ships with all the flags I had memorized in sixth-grade geography. It was said there were movie stars in a place called Malibu, and people who spoke another language, came from Mexico, and lived across a river on the other side of Downtown.

All this seemed improbable. There were no rivers in Los Angeles. In any event, my divisions were human in dimension, feet and yards and miles.

I lived on Sepulveda Boulevard, in interchangeable apartments resembling intrinsically shabby barracks. They were minimal in all the wrong ways. Even the foliage was uniform and boring, rubber trees and oleander, green at the edges with an absence of startling deviation. They could have planted orchids and trumpet vines, but didn't. They could have constructed edifices of glass and terraces, with fountains adorning courtyards and tile plazas, but didn't. That would have been an un-American statement, a tangible admission that our nature didn't need to be beaten into submission. But that was beyond the national expectation and vision. It would have been heretical and subversive.

Our Los Angeles was a version of the indigenous subdued, easy to mow, fast growing, with vegetation requiring as little water or attention as possible. It was an insignificant afterthought, a perimeter in lime chalk, meant to be erased. Still, we adhered to the national craving for conformity. It was the era of 2.2 children, station wagons, just enough lawn to resonate symbolically, tract houses and planned communities.

Los Angeles was a sketchy half-built haphazard captured piece of desert, and to call it tropical was a mass dissimulation, a contagious hallucination. Saint Vitus' dance and witch burnings are not aberrations but routine outbreaks of an intrinsic cultural malaria. Los Angeles fevered and shivered. By 1960, it was already disintegrating, though no one seemed to protest. Quiet streets, few cars, and fines for littering.

The apartments where I grew up were so nearly identical, I checked the row numbers against the key I wore around my neck to be certain I had returned to my designated walkway between stucco. The apartments faced fields like muddy camouflage where heavy machinery one day just appeared. They were constructing the ultimate highway, right down to the Mexican border. Or perhaps it was going to Sydney or Shanghai.

It had nothing to do with my life, which was linear, straight as Sepulveda or Santa Monica or Pico boulevards, curving down to sun-drained pockets of ocean at Santa Monica Bay. My childhood was summers of walking to the beach, searching for glass soda bottles to be redeemed for two or three cents each. You found them under the Santa Monica Pier. Vagrants slept beneath the pilings and planks, and children had been molested and beaten there. But we were thirsty, urban primitives with a limited repertoire.

Survival was a constant sequence of strategies to accumulate another day. We found bottles in gutters and vacant lots beneath fronds and jacaranda petals fallen on cement, curled like a multitude of severed purple ears gradually fermenting. We often cut ourselves, even when using sticks in hunting and gathering our armful of glass.

I was a girl child of the already decomposing streets of a Los Angeles that harbored concealed slums, inland ports not on the nautical charts. It was a city of divisions based on accents, dialects, race, religious affiliations, and, of course, money. The Mexicans were called beaners and greasers. Asians were Buddhaheads.

There was nothing remarkable about the undifferentiated neighborhood named West Los Angeles in 1960. In the montage of mutations and fictions I call

memory, the inhabitants of this nouveau feudal kingdom also arrived not by choice, but by catastrophe.
My neighbors came for their health, the promise of
no winter where your survival odds were statistically
better. This Los Angeles was the consolation prize in
the final lottery. It's where the Greyhound stopped.

This was before Seattle, Santa Fe, Denver, Austin,
and Atlanta. Los Angeles was where you came after
going broke in Baltimore or Milwaukee. It was where
you went after scandal. It was a frontier with castes,
the lower rungs occupied by certain women we were
forbidden to speak to, divorcees and single mothers, though that term hadn't yet been codified. It was
still a country that asserted the natural order was a
male and female cohabiting with their biological offspring. This was the sacred configuration, intrinsic,
implacable, and it would never change.

My childhood had a quality of stigma and words
that couldn't be uttered. The poverty one didn't speak
of, the diseases one didn't dare name, and the family
dysfunctions, the symptoms and behaviors one never
mentioned. The father who gambled, the sister who
ran away, the mother with a nervous breakdown.

The deliberately dreary housing reinforced dazed
submission. Resignation was the norm. *Alcoholism*
and *cancer* and *divorce* were still sordid words and
rumored to be spread through the air. To utter such
syllables was considered foul. Spells and incantations lingered as plausible explanations among the

populace. It went without saying, and should not be questioned, that diseases were afflictions coming directly and randomly from God. They were meant to be suffered. In this respect, it is interesting to note the controversy centered on supplying terminal patients with agony-alleviating narcotics. The AMA did not approve and authorize pain-reduction methods until the 1980s. Of course, educational opportunities were determined by obvious socioeconomic factors. Piano lessons and orthodontists belonged to another species. Exile contains visual and auditory components beyond the obvious.

There are implications in the minimalist architecture and landscaping that occur to me now. Apartments lacking insulation but possessing an obligatory balcony with regulation pink geraniums, petals soiled by sun and chemical pollution. The flower pot like a burnt prop that spoke of some fundamental violation. The anemic geranium in need of an exorcism.

Wasn't Los Angeles always a sort of massive studio set, a clever assemblage of façades, of what appear to be buildings but actually have no foundations or interiors beyond what the camera demands? Didn't it always have a posthumous ghost-town quality, with a few plants scattered about as if for set design? Weren't we all bit players, summoned when a crowd shot was to be filmed?

Our designated residences were arranged in military order, regimented and regulated. Later, presumably, we would be standing in lines for food stamps and welfare checks, probation officers and prisons. Get used to it now.

They were constructing freeways but they weren't for us. There was a global agenda that also had nothing to do with the people who actually lived here, rode buses when they had enough dimes, hung their sheets between barbed fences and trees of hard avocados like so many dark green stones.

There were two distinct configurations in this Southern California basin. The assembly of little neighborhoods where we, the indigenous population, lived, and lived poorly, hungry, shabby, and frightened. We were the offspring of disaster, personal, sociological, and climatic, the residue from failed families and farms, the legacy of sharecroppers, Mexican harvest workers, Asian refugees, and European ghettos. And we came to Los Angeles for the great American promise of a second chance.

And there was the city of myth they were building around and through us. This was the city of buzz and even we could hear it. The city of dream, of tycoons and scantily clothed movie stars in organ-shaped pink swimming pools in the hills, some hills, somewhere. This other new Los Angeles was distant as San Diego or Honolulu. The not-yet-built city of the future was for another group of people entirely. We walked between used cars that broke repeatedly and hung our sheets in gritty insolent sun, but we were shadowy and unnecessary. The potential infrastructure, kept in reserve, in limbo, just in case we proved economically viable later.

We were less than bit players in the larger incomprehensible scheme. We'd never have speaking lines, costumes, or be paid union scale. That's what our cynically indifferent architecture told us. This was a kind of boot camp, some precarious extension of the Greyhound parking lot, a void where you repacked your bedroll and bandaged your feet. The sooner we left, the better.

We were already in the way. Our tract houses were razed for freeways. The city ordered this. They had a master plan. The new Los Angeles selected for another breed. You didn't come here because your daughter had asthma or they foreclosed your hardware store in Iowa. You came for another climate and it had nothing to do with temperature. It wasn't about the absence of blizzards and black ice, but power and money. The new enterprises with their potent fuel of images and sounds, the record and movie companies, real estate and investment, fashion and stardom. Still later, such alliances of cartels and coalitions would be known as industries.

It was before lunching stylishly replaced dialogue and sensibility as an art form. Los Angeles as she was before her innumerable cosmetic procedures, the creative hair and makeup stylists, elocution lessons, manicures, implants, and braces. It was before she became the city that opened her personal trainer sculpted white legs to the arriving regiments of the narcissistic personality disorder. It wasn't yet a city of mirrors with an audio track in a perpetual loop, a two-word mantra that said *love me, love me, love me.*

My Los Angeles was a second-rate southern fishing village, a border town with a drawl. It was an enormous trailer park on sand, something anomalous storms had brought, and we were beached and stranded. We moved slow. We caught starved gray bonito from the pier and walked barefoot on streets where we did not yet have drive-by shootings or multinational entertainment conglomerates. Culver City and Mar Vista were distinct as feudal kingdoms. Downtown itself was a distant abstraction. We only went there on field trips.

I'm not surprised that Los Angeles has replaced New York as the flagship city in crisis at the millennium. I witnessed my hometown become synonymous with urban obsolescence and all that implies, anarchy, brutal indiscriminate violence, and an absence of consensual values and motivation.

Now that I observe Los Angeles from my apple orchard in the Allegheny Mountains, the cause and effect are obvious. As the mythic allure of Los Angeles dissipates, as technology makes it viable to live in Maui or Telluride or even here, in this village between Pittsburgh and Toronto, it's like the gigantic set is being struck. They've packed away the costumes, crated up the props, and bits of stage design. Computer graphics made such three-dimensional manifestations unnecessary. Los Angeles has no artifacts, only debris.

And I know the Los Angeles that's been left behind. It's the Los Angeles that was always there. A city of the disadvantaged, ignored, and dismissed. The invisible legions inhabiting the anonymous outskirts and back streets enameled by sun while the city of dream came and is now departing.

Now it's the land of the children of the bit players and there's nothing virtual about them. They are real and they are angry. They never liked their bad acid trip cheap motel-like apartments emblazoned with insults in six languages, gang logos gauged by knives on walls and doors, windows latticed with metal bars. Through ripped mesh, stepfathers and boyfriends verbally abuse the girls, syllables of degradation ricochet in sand and salt breeze like hand grenades that are internalized. Some words become scars in neural networks, swallowed land mines, exploding from within.

The skies look like a battlefield. You can mutilate yourself standing on a patio at sunset. And now many of their progeny are drugged and armed. In a town that makes even supermodels want to commit suicide, they've breathed all the cactus splinters and adobe dust they can. They're over the measurable legal limit. They're the progeny of demolished for shopping malls, tract houses that came for another chance and didn't get it. They longed for a moment in the sun and got radiation burns and melanoma instead.

These are the children of single women, spending their weekends with blinds closed to shut out alleys of scorched oleander, abandoned market baskets, and trash entwined in dried stylistically insignificant vegetation. On the boulevards below, any vehicle can contain AK-47s. They're the potential infrastructure, the contingency plan locked in storage, now generations beyond divorce.

On Sunday afternoons, the women sew buttons and repair hems with nervous hands. They assemble quarters for the bus. They smoke cigarettes and their hands shake. You know what they're thinking? I'll tell you. This is a region of abscesses not mentioned in the guidebooks where everyday is another audition with a casting couch.

The Los Angeles that remains is populated by their offspring, the children of citrus too spoiled to pick and the bus like a blue lifeline in a city without trains, taxis, or trams. The children of earthquake damage that hasn't been repaired yet and probably never will. The fault lines aren't just on maps. They infiltrate into the subconscious, creating internal plateaus and mesas of nightmares enacted against a backdrop of graffiti encrusted cul-de-sacs. Where they live, you need a password to get in and a miracle to get out.

It isn't that Los Angeles suddenly changed. It's rather that the virtual Los Angeles is fading. The trade winds have shifted. They don't last for centuries like they used to. Constantinople. Thebes. Genoa. We cruise at 40,000 feet now, 600 mph, and even the wind isn't important. The last ships from the temporary colony are sailing away. They're not saying good-bye, either.

And the Los Angeles that was always here, growing silently, breeding and molting, fermenting under an incendiary sun is finally daring to stir. The spawn of hillsides of wild succulents opening under a lid of sky chemical reactions turn into gulfs and canals of lurid brandy are reaching hands through bamboo. They stand above freeway embankments the khaki of camouflage. They're through having numbers rather than names and waiting for crew to call them in. Some stains are visual hieroglyphics that do not require translation.

There's an alchemy that inspires recognition with a Glock. Within the stucco-coated rooms, locked guarded courtyards, and barricaded cul-de-sacs, it is worse. No one seems to have noticed outrage seething in the seemingly silent occupied population. But we never believed their homogeneous slogans and propaganda. We weren't getting speaking lines. We weren't part of their empire. And in truth, we've been in an extremely agitated mood and methodically preparing for insurrection for at least a generation.

Transmission to Los Angeles #5

$\mathcal{W}$HEN SNOW FALLS FOR SEVEN OR eight consecutive months, and the forest is a spectrum of relentless gray, I know what I miss most about Los Angeles. It's not sun setting over the bluffs of Santa Monica Bay in a sequence of 82-degree days framed by palms and hibiscus. What I crave, while black ice falls for weeks at a stretch, are the shopping malls.

The shopping malls of Los Angeles are the ultimate manifestation of the architecture of consumption. They assure a known and protected environment with a recognizable purpose. They are our form of a sanctified public area, a commons or town square. And you don't need permission, don't have to show your ID, visa, or pay for admission.

In a shopping mall there is the promise of discovery and reinvention. You enter the monumental entranceways as one must have the gates of the Coliseum, passing armed guards and statues of warriors and gods. Here, all things are possible, rare entertainments from distant points of the empire, trinkets and amulets and the not implausible possibility of a public display of blood. It's the beginning of the safari, the tracking, the hunt, and adventure of outwitting global merchandising conspiracies. You directly confront the forces of international marketing. You don't need lances or high-grade explosives. You have a more powerful object, the charge card.

Time stops in the mall. You recognize certain stores like mountain peaks or rivers on maps. These are your compass points in the enclosed structured environment. Shopping malls offer a sense of uniformity and anonymity that is reassuring. It's like a bureaucratic embrace. The twenty-first century is actually happening, of course, but not to you, personally. In Los Angeles, where one feels involved in all major events, where we feel we *are* the larger culture, the mall relieves us of our special status. We are all small and ordinary in the uniform corridors between tiers of steel girders, winding stairways, and lobbies with atriums. That's an integral part of the beauty of the experience. We manage to escape ourselves.

Of course, special attire is required. Jogging outfits, sunglasses, and baseball caps. It's the look cleverly designed to give the appearance that we are, in fact, celebrities attempting to pass incognito. Since almost everyone is dressed this way, would-be actresses and screenwriters currently doing secretarial temp work, housewives, Grammy nominees, and gang members, only you know how unique you actually are.

In the mall, all we fear is held in remission. The

lighting, temperature, and scents are designed and controlled. The incessant assault of nights thick with vines like upended kelp studded with ocean pearls implying strangulation rather than ceremonial adornment, are banished. The lemon and orange trees, the used-up ocean of poisonous fish and debris, the riots, whatever war our government is currently inflicting in whatever nation or time zone, none of that matters. We enter a stylized version of the future. We understand this because it tells us what we already know. We are not cynics. But we are pragmatic. The bottom line is that you can buy your way in or out of anything.

There are subtle seasons in the malls of Los Angeles. Geography is translated, vetted by focus groups, and manufactured. Seasons appear where there are none. Christmas smells of tinny piano music and men's charcoal sweaters with wide red ribbons around them. It's a Christmas you feel with your fingers, silk and cashmere. Everything is black velvet and brass, tiny beaded evening bags and purses encrusted with bangles and mirrors. We are in gala red mode through Valentine's Day. We think of high heels, beads that dangle, hearts in the shape of purses, necklaces, and acres of scarves printed with lipstick kisses. It's still the holiday season and anyone with a credit card can go to the ball. The malls of Los Angeles are utterly egalitarian.

The season of shopping-mall red begins just after

summer and ends in February. It's a magical red, like an old-fashioned movie-theater curtain. It's a red achieved by simulating sounds, lighting, and fragrances. It's a subliminal appeal to childhood memory. It's a satin-ribbon red seen on early Christmas mornings by children wearing flannel. It's a synergistic red, part suggestion, free association, and a complicated manipulation done with lightbulbs and the folds of fabrics that mimic velvet. It's the definitive 8 a.m. of crumpled wrapping paper you want to repeat forever. It's a fabricated memory of a Christmas you probably never had, a sophisticated amalgam of implants you suspect is artificial but still crave. In the shopping mall, it's always a morning to open your presents. It's always time for dress up. There is an implication you can even buy your way back to normal.

In the background, epic sound-track music insinuates itself between steel retrofitted girders. Themes from spectacular motion pictures remind you of how someone's heart might beat as he rides a camel across a Saharan desert. Something is rising from sand, suggesting drums pushing out of concrete, a tribal dance beneath your feet, and you are agile and fertile again. If you purchase the right jacket, you can spend the day with Sean Connery or Paul Newman as they once were and remain in celluloid untainted forever. Outside, it's an afternoon the blue of Bob Dylan's eyes and in the mall, there is no tarnish, only an intimation of bells and their graceful afterimages. There are mirrors and you look thin in all of them.

It's a constant vanilla-scented softly lit early afternoon in an indeterminate season of no consequence. The sun does not intimidate, raw and coarse. It is tamed, held behind a complex architecture of concrete-covered walls decorated for every conceivable occasion. In the perennial delirium of buying season, it's a permanent holiday.

There is always reason to purchase perfume. Bottles and vials with French and Greek words on them, so much scent it's like a powder or gas in your lungs. Perfumes with pseudoscientific names like *Antigen* or *Oncogene*. Who cares what it means? It sounds like the millennium and essences of a superpower. Who knows what ingredients are added to these potents? Perhaps you will smell like rain forests at noon and also be immune to cancer. Purchasing a bottle is a token admission into the corporate global mechanism, like a share of stock.

And between the epic sound tracks, behind blocks of glossy simulated brass, Styrofoam snowflakes, and enormous steel red painted Valentine's Day hearts, come the Mother's Day pastel garlands. They are fashioned from some material that will outlive you and your descendents. Frank Sinatra is singing "Strangers in the Night" and "New York, New York." Metallic fibers are embedded in the stylized artificial snow and flowers. It's the sort of sparkle a person can count on. We don't care if these materials are biodegradable. There's a certain solace in knowing these constructions will live longer than you or your loves or even the concept of love itself. There's an implication you're participating effectively in the collective planet development. As you shop, you are laying bricks for the foundation of the future, whatever that is.

Of course, the malls of Los Angeles are, at their core, about love. How we can drape ourselves to lure and keep it, how we can tangibly demonstrate our affection by what we purchase and give. In my memory, the malls are filled with stores named *Compulsion* and *Eternal Longing, Fantastic Addiction, Conflagration, Blazing Ardor,* and *Absolute Vice.* This is a psychological terrain you walk three or four levels through, simultaneously stupefied and wildly alert. A delusion with elevators and food courts where taped birds chirp. Demarcations of hours and seasons dissolve. It's the arrested moment of consumer love. It's a persistent shopping soft amber tinged with invisible cigarette smoke, and aromatic skin creams with names suggesting smuggled gold and leathers that caress. Bottles contain distilled essences of passion and experimental gene therapy. You can purchase fluid incantations and alter your molecular structure. It's a dream you don't want to have or wake up from. It's an alternative reality.

At such junctures, I felt I was finally learning how

to dream in English. It's a neon language, excessively and aggressively visual. Everything is a sexual shorthand rendered in insatiable crimson and brass, a focus group's version of an exhaustion-induced trance. You are simultaneously overly stimulated and subdued. To understand this dialect you must be vertical, walking or riding an escalator. You must hold shopping bags embossed with internationally acclaimed designer initials. They are the new global warlords. We carry items with their imprint to ensure ourselves safe passage. It's our twenty-first-century passport.

In the background, behind plastic palms, imitation snowflakes, or Mother's Day bouquets composed of searing acrylic, the music is constantly and chaotically changing. From movie themes you find yourself in a shop shaking from the mix of rhythms and styles called world beat. It's an auditory initiation offered in an evolving patois, a millennial conjunction more frantic than any known dialect. Everything is jittery as if on amphetamines, punctuated by neon, and a scent like spiced ginger and genetically engineered almond that says *buy me.*

While the mall has indisputable holiday demarcations, the known corridors where Frank Sinatra sings or hip-hop dominates, there are the sudden inspirations of special events and the thrill of Sale Days. This is an enchanted season of the mall, unpredictable, like a celestial aberration, perhaps, an earthquake or typhoon.

Sale Days occur randomly, like acts of nature, acts of despots, or acts of love. We have grown to expect this, how the ordinary equations suddenly vanish. Sale Days have their own clarity, their singular white laser light. On Sale mornings, or Half-Off Saturdays, we approach the mall as if on a pilgrimage. We will find the ability to conceive of generosity in a larger framework. The past becomes manageable. We understand that grace and the fortuitous are as possible as cataclysm. On Sale Days, anything can happen.

I enter the monumental edifice, eager for discovery. Something about the nature of man will be revealed. After all, we are barbarians with charge cards instead of clubs. In the airports and train stations of all capitals, booths sell transparent underwear and Radiohead CDs. We seem to be moving too slowly for our lives, barely crawling across the tiles, dragging our designer shopping bags and bad childhoods with us. We ride the elevators in silence. It's the day of the aftermath. But we have survived and retain our capacity for the festive. Sale Days suggest resurrection and rebirth. It's a sort of face-lift without the pain or expense of surgery. We can start over and we can do it at half price.

Revelation is possible anywhere, not merely in plazas with plaques denoting sacred events and on monuments etched with the headlines of centuries. One need not stand on the mossy cliffs of jungle-side

Maui at sunset, in a wash of mauve and violet, to see the earth's heart beat.

On Sale Day, in the house wares department of Macy's or Bloomingdale's, I am ready. I stalk the crystal section, holding fluted goblets, and wineglasses with gold around the rims and diamond patterns along the sides. I stare at vases for all occasions, noting how they appear encrusted with jewels. I decipher this bold assertion. It can be coronation day in your living room every day. Do you have the money?

I stand near candlestick holders and votive sets shaped like stars and fans, blossoms and hearts, pairs of them, as if they were married. Would I feel the burden of so much illumination? If I purchase a set and then a vase, wouldn't the ordinary world prove a disappointment? How could I ever be celebratory enough to maintain this level of gala? There would be the constant necessity for flower arrangements and candlelight. And the commitment to elegance and appearance of psychological discipline and control. Even if everything went right, my marriage, my daughter, the multinational economic forces, the coalitions of corporations in shifting alliances, the subterranean impulses of governments and the human heart, would such objects require additional emotional obligations? Is it too much responsibility? Is it the wrong statement?

On Sale Day, when rebirth is at your fingertips,

the forces of selection weigh heavy on your back. There are impulses your hands resist. You can afford the items, yes. But what they imply is dizzying. The political assertions. Are they correct enough? The self-definition on display, solid and unassailable. Some objects present challenges of unexpected and unnecessary exposure. There are moments when there is no line between enlightenment and a debilitating migraine.

In the silver section, it's an eternal celebration in sterling. What could one possibly serve on trays embossed with angels and birds? Let's face it. There is nothing I could ever do with crackers, cheese, and cantaloupe slices to answer this tray with silver villages sculpted on the edges. Could I ever eat enough for this? Could I be creative enough with a knife? Do I have the genetic and environmental resources for the presentation such objects demand?

There are more questions in the alcove of silver gift frames. It's been hours on the trail now. I sense the sun going down, even if I can't actually see it behind the next generation Space Age walls, and the passageways studded with enclosed aviaries and battery-operated birds. But there is no more time for ambivalence. This is the definitive moment. Sale Day has a clearly defined end.

Yes. I have photographs worthy of tangible display. It is 70 percent off on silver frames with satin finish, silver frames with nouveau lilies, with silver doves and roses, bells and twining grapevines. I buy three. I am saying, yes, our lives are worthy. Our 26" trout from the Snake River is worthy. Yes, our sailing jaunt to Catalina, how we looked windblown and brown, surprised to have not drowned. Our tent in the Anza Borrego beside a stream strewn with willow leaves where howling coyotes in packs chased rabbits through our camp sight at night. Us, formal for the Oscar's, once. And our daughter, then, now, and always, her piano recitals, horseback rides, skis and roller blades. And perhaps there will be additional moments to preserve. Her college graduation, perhaps. Her courtships and eventual marriage. The possibility of grandchildren.

Somewhere, Frank Sinatra is singing "Strangers in the Night." I breathe in vanilla, air an ambered filigree, a mist of votives and clandestine initiations. It might be May or November, midmorning or night. Malls are constructed from materials designed to last one hundred thousand years during which sounds combined from tribal drums, mariachis, string quartets, and synthesizers will continue playing. There are fabrics from Nepal, Borneo, and Peru. Tapestries from Turkey and Prague. And items that imply black-market intrigue and illicit barges crossing night rivers in areas of jungle combat. One thinks of warlords and concubines, alchemy and contraband.

In a single Sale Day in a mall in Los Angeles, I saw the unfolding and dissection of history. I battled multinational cartels and federations of corporations for my dollars. I stalked half-price prey in the camouflaged artificial, not day or night, shopping-mall focus group endorsed yellow. Is it surprising that a woman returning from such an expedition requires aspirin and absolute silence?

It is this adventure that I miss. It's not the trophies themselves, the tangible victory of the hunt, or even the way sensibility can be distilled into a 5″ × 7″ silver frame. It is rather that the malls of Los Angeles are our version of the archetypical bazaar, our souk. They are our translation of Alexandria and Rome.

Here, in the interminable Allegheny Mountain winter, I remember that great trading cities were ports, ocean and sea and river. It is on such waters that ambiguous substances and science, spices and antiquities, contraband and relics were transported. Philosophers and bards, priests and magicians, and men and women exiled for ideas pronounced heretical traveled such waters. Outlaws and eccentrics censored in their area codes who would later be pronounced visionaries and geniuses. It is in this spirit that I'm from Los Angeles, the last outpost of the other century and first port of the new.

Transmission to Los Angeles
#6

$\mathcal{S}$INCE I'M MANIC-DEPRESSIVE, TECH-
nically bipolar II with many border-
line features, the ferocity of these extreme Allegheny
seasons tend to stun and disorient me. I stagger and
drift into wildly different personalities as winds and
sun shift.

Snowed in for weeks, I have the time and inclination to reconsider Los Angeles, particularly as my
hometown. It's not revisionism or nostalgia, but a
continuing synthesis. I now see my hometown with
the singular clarity that, ironically, is possible only by
absence. It's an affection that stems from a lens that
magnifies and clarifies.

Los Angeles and I came of age together. To actually claim Los Angeles as your city of birth or choice
is a brazen admission. It puts you on the defensive,
immediately and permanently. We didn't have art,
of course, but rather some secondary and tawdry
subspecies, the film industry. As if that wasn't stain
enough, we then encouraged an even more degener-
ate relative, the music business.

But there was more. It had something to do with

that indigenous non-Eastern seaboard flora, and the insistence of Spain's Gold Coast itself demanding recognition. After generations of gray stone cities, we were a riot of magenta bougainvillea, an astonishment of canna, May and June a sudden onslaught of purple jacaranda, rampant eruptions of renegade divas in silky petals, arias and pearls.

In retrospect, it's inexplicable that the sheer dazzle of this city could have been so curiously and perversely misunderstood. Rather than recognizing Los Angeles as breathtaking and original, a Mae West of cities, brassy, seminal, brilliant, and boldly defiant, we were considered vulgar, common, and deficient. We were what you found after the impassable mountains, marauding desperados, tribes who spoke other languages, and canyons spiked with inedible cactus.

It was a domestic conspiracy, comparing Los Angeles to established Eastern cities and pronouncing us lacking. The rabbit-pulled-out-of-a-hat-in-reverse trick. We were so avant-garde we seemed invisible, an embarrassment of absence. No publishing, ballet, or Ivy League schools. We didn't have taxis. We didn't even have rain.

Time gave us our credibility. There were revisions and the world caught up. Rather than an infected aberration, Los Angeles anchored the Sunbelt. Logically, Los Angeles would be the prototypical twenty-first-century city. At its core, it's a World War II phenomenon, built by young men who crossed the Pacific as soldiers. As Californians, Tokyo and Mexico City are closer points of reference, of high art and style, than Europe. Our Lady, Queen of the Angels, always thought in global terms. Our Lady of irrefutably modernistic assumptions, decreeing speed and distance and technology as givens, permanent and intrinsic, part of the grain itself. A young city, gracefully vulnerable and unrepentantly flexible. An anticity, really, defiant and prophetic.

Other notions drifted under the palms and deceptively celadon sunsets. Radical ideas floated beside ridges of canna and oleander. Something was coalescing in the burgundy-laced dusk. Neighborhoods, the cornerstone of American life, were becoming obsolete. Movement had become part of the American psyche. The future would be a manifestation of the self in transition, determined by districts of affinities and aesthetics.

There was a deliberate statement of purpose in what Los Angeles didn't have. We are not only what we do, but also what we refuse to do. Without the recognizable pavilions of certification and display, Los Angeles dared assert that art might not be just objects for purchase and accumulation, but an organic human process, constantly growing, mutating, perhaps, alongside lemon and orange groves, eviscerated by sun.

Without the prescribed fortresses, sanctified battlegrounds and palaces of what a city is supposed to be, Los Angeles offered a blasphemous premise. It was a public evolution. It took decades to acquire museums and theaters, and in between, Los Angeles was pinned in lacerating afternoons, raw and vulnerable. Los Angeles, the last protectorate of the old trade route and first of the new.

After Death Valley and Donner Pass, after the wagon trains, talkies and radio, decades of dust, and multifarious migrations, one finally reached the final coast. You stand on a bluff above the Pacific, waves below the slow blues of absolution. There are resolutions, after all. Glance over your shoulder and it occurs to you that the entire twenty-first century has proved to be a suburb of Los Angeles.

By its nature, a still coalescing city offers a fragile anatomy, brittle and illusive. It rises on heretical assumptions. It says cities aren't eternal; their structures are transitional and improvisational. It is only desert and ocean that ultimately remain. You must invent your own rituals of passage, celebration, and solace.

The Los Angeles I miss no longer exists. As befits an evolving city, the bungalows, houses, and lofts where I lived and sometimes loved have largely disappeared, bulldozed into shopping malls, freeways, and pieces incorporated into office and apartment complexes. It's been swallowed, discarded, and rewoven.

I retain an aching affection for Pacific Ocean Park. In the early '60s, a manikin Neptune waved his phosphorescent trident from a seashell-strewn elevator/grotto on a pier in Santa Monica. There I first conceived of fishnets as possible decor items, fabrics to be strung on walls or worn on the legs. At Pacific Ocean Park, or POP, one could ride in a transparent plastic bubble skyway, a cable across yards of semidark beach. I had my first thirteen-year-old kiss suspended above shallow waves, headlights on the highway behind like the illuminated perimeter, and it occurred to me that boundaries can be crossed, tunneled under, flown over, and eradicated.

I feel a lingering affection for the romanticism of the '60s, the love-ins and be-ins in Griffith Park, lyrical medieval inspirations in groves with stages as we lay on blankets beneath eucalyptus and pines. Jimi Hendrix and Janis Joplin performing under a scattering of stars at the Greek Theater and Hollywood Bowl. Dusk was Haight Ashbury velvet blue. I wanted a jacket made from such a fabric. I'd stitch sequins in shapes of constellations across the cuffs in rooms of smoky indigo where stanzas were read out loud, marijuana passed mouth to mouth, and words mattered. Exploring consciousness was a sacred rite, a citizen's obligation. I don't know how these examinations became degraded and officially outlawed. But that was later.

The Doors were the house band at the Whisky. The Sunset Strip had a brief flirtation with coffeehouse underground high art, poetry with bongo drums, and jazz, before surrendering to strip clubs and fast-food joints. My veins were still the blue bus lines and my accouterments were contained in a single canvas bag, my sandals, transistor radio, sunglasses, paperbacks, cigarettes, and change.

The defining characteristic of a hometown is that it's the landscape of childhood. Los Angeles remains inviolate, the shape and texture of innocence. I am a younger version, too, my sundress of strawberries vivid pink, pulsating. A mysterious process, a quantum gap, and the rows of uniform shabby apartments, windows behind bars in soiled afternoons, obligatory balconies piled with the rusting splintered rubble of fractured ambitions flicker, like a kite, a votive. If no one saw us, were we here?

It is my hometown I stand as all children, small and awed. There are no mortgages, traffic congestion, cancer, corruption, heartbreak, no unexpected diagnosis, death, or divorce. The sky is rendered flawless to the horizon, not midnight or cobalt or powder blue, not turquoise or aqua or any blue that can be named or spoken by a human mouth. It's the texture of prayer, perhaps. The ocean is subterranean corridors, serpentine and violet, breeding their own kinetic dialects.

You walk out your door and this is what you see. One textbook-perfect fan palm like an organic statue erected on a bluff above a stretch of amethyst Pacific. In winter, poinsettias emerge like red mouths above coves. They might want to bite or kiss you.

When snow melts, the spring flowers rise, apple trees bud in startled overnight white, starched and fragile and I realize I've survived another Allegheny winter. The earth smells alive again, after the antiseptic ice, like it's just woken from suspended animation or a coma, and I remember Los Angeles.

I know this with certainty. Los Angeles broke my heart. But you can't find these fissures on regulation Southern California maps. We crossed the entire country for this tawdry one-time fishing village suspended on the rumored trade route of the next millennium. I know. It happened to me. It happened to millions of us.

There was the symbolic trek across gashes of desert with no ground or horizon, air neutral and camouflaged. No system of measurement applied, too many ashes, too many lies. Along the 3,000 miles of ache, I saw cottonwoods beside irrigation canals, willows near rivers, blue spruce and aspen in alpine meadows, and none of it mattered or spoke. Perhaps it was encrypted. Refugees in flight rarely take photographs or make notations on the sides of pages. Annotation comes later, a procedure that can gut and consume a lifetime.

I did not arrive at Stateline, with fluorescent casinos in sand like tower beacons, but rather accidentally chanced to survive. Then acres of orchards, date palms in lines above tumbleweeds and roads crisscrossing shadowy valley floors like the angular streets you might follow into some irredeemable internal exile. On the sides of highways were hedges of defiled pink hibiscus. I would not put such flowers in my hair. They would stain me with their sullen beaten pink. I wondered if this was all California had to teach me.

Los Angeles was rusting shells of terraces superimposed on tentative two-story apartments, courtyards that seemed deserted where parched plants were immolated by sun. This was the DNA. You did not need to be a molecular biologist or poet to decode this stilted helix. Seagulls circled above drying sheets. The ocean was salty through deformed citrus worms would reject. Outside was a flat plain in circus colors and boulevards that were not serious with names like Wavecrest, Pier, Breeze, Pacific, and Marine. Who did they think they were kidding?

In winter, the San Gabriel Mountains were snow capped, casting a cold gloss across the basin of flat rectangular intersections. They were a pathetic and intrinsically mediocre geometry. That's what I learned in high school. Then the suburbs with aggressively intimidating repetitions like block cities designed by malevolent children. I understood this and how the air reeked of abandonment, chaos, and neglect.

My childhood was increments of stucco, sequences of renegade miles in a frontier of gaudy burgundy dusk, and too much orange leaking from the sky and rising from the pavement. These streets remain after experiment and ruin. This is what the ground refuses.

Desert winds blow, charged Santa Anas, a confluence of flame and sand. It is abstract, obsolete, and eternal. It has memorized the rituals of owls and bobcats in arroyos. It could tell you stories about acts of insolence and supplication, but you must know how to listen. If I became fluent in this occult dialect, they would punish me.

I believed there was a kind of logic in this, a stunted progression. It was there, in the rank texture of palms, trunks wind etched and indecipherable. I held my breath. I took an imaginary picture. I called it noon and choked.

My adolescence was afternoons of light absolutely absorbed, rubbed away past intention. Such sun seemed lacquered, thick, the texture of paint. It was simultaneously combative, languid, and depressed.

There was no innocence to lose on this coast of tainted bougainvillea listless in brass afternoons of no seasons where the young men were dying. That was later. The time of a plague called AIDS. A war was occurring within the cells and blood of relatives, colleagues, and friends. A suspicious disease without a cure, more a murmured rumor than a fact, was killing young men. There was suffering, fear, and death with burials like battles where causality figures astound as decimated regiments do. But these deaths didn't get citations and parades.

Los Angeles was warehouses of impossibilities, residues of trial and error, risks both desperate and gratuitous. A construct like a sound stage containing an entire tiled plaza with a wide-open morgue, public like an exhibit, an archive. Here were shelves with all the wrong doors, the ones we should have never opened, crossed the prairies or Donner Pass. It was the last desperate chance and maybe it shouldn't have been taken. In burning buildings some chose not to jump through glass but inhale the smoke instead. Who knows what they think then? That the flame is their ineluctable destiny? Or intervention will somehow be sent, like an answered prayer? Or perhaps they are simply too bewildered and exhausted to take action.

I have come to know this singular terrain with an intimacy not entirely voluntary. Always, palms stand on cliffs above Santa Monica Bay, motionless in dusk, beneath sudden glazed gulfs stained lavender and aerial avenues of red. Soon there will be no centers. Sun sets in an orange so hard it's like watching the detonation of a hydrogen bomb and the fallout is falling on you. It's not night but ground zero.

This cannot be the reason we crossed mountain ranges and deserts. Not for this hillbilly hooker who thinks she's Marilyn Monroe and plans to get into pictures. Not for this no-grammar gal with six weeks of Berlitz she calls learning French. The one who knows it's just about getting them to open the right doors, meet the right people, the ones with the power to alter your trajectory with a single telephone call. If you find the right soda fountain, shoes, or hairstyle, rebirth is possible. They'll buy you new teeth and erase your accent. Hey, what are you waiting for? Step up to the green felt table, kid. Put your chip down and spin the wheel, toss the dice. Anyone can get lucky.

So this is Los Angeles, this deluded accidental seaside village on the edge of the new Space Age trade route. This is the first port of the future and what does she say? *Want any crack* in Chinese, in Thai, Vietnamese, Spanish, Armenian, Russian, and Farsi.

One thing is certain. Night is cold. Vines responsive to the moon open along alleys where darkness is scented and drunken. Air turns a fantastic blue, perfumed and bruised between fronds of palms. Such a blue intimates not grace but rather a promise vast and extravagant and utterly squandered.

Now I return a decade later. The waters of this Santa Monica Bay are fragile blue, translucent as the skin of abused infants. I think of insomnia and fever, of some ancient confusion that lingers. They claim to have healed this bay, but certain residues contain half-lives and are permanent.

Last week, morning was elegant, ocean a suggestion of bleached iris like a stamp on an antique passport where you see ink being eaten by air. There is a tattooed quality in this breeze, some impossible to eradicate port sense of ocean and its possibilities.

At midnight, I heard bells from a ship or cathedral. A requiem or consecration? Waves were like
inverted rain, horizontal fluids trying to rise in re-
verse, defy gravity and engineer their own resurrection. This was once called the city of dream.

Villages of the insane and consensually banished appear on dusk sand. Why not? This is where
America stopped. But it is temporary, a mild intermittent fever or mirage. In the pre-dawn, the authori-
ties, representatives of the current interpretation of
order, sweep the beach of debris, the transitory tin
and canvas clutter of the homeless. The multitudes
without walls, without visas, and the documents,
the charge cards and numbers that prove legitimate
existence. The ocean is light and gauzy then; air fills
with a fine sea dust, a faint taste of spices and opium,
perfumes and precious metals in wooden crates on
sandy floors veiled beneath shallows.

Beyond this are the dilapidated canals; paths over-
grown with vines and embankments of startled red
geraniums. I tried to understand why this particular
city was once called revelatory, even holy. I watched
waves break in lines like fingers, like the many arms
of deities rising from regions known only from leg-
end. They bloom in dusk by certain oceans where
the trade routes have been and gone. They have their
own seasons and angles of manifestation. You might
have already found and failed to notice their delicate
assertions. Or perhaps they were in remission as you

passed, and you missed them completely. You tossed the dice and lost.

I realized how similar variations of the same theme are, here in the post-tropics, in the indistinct ruins of early Pacific Rim cities. Inland, women stand in plazas, exposed in a light mist, languid and stunned. They have lost their ivory combs and mantillas, their medallions robbed or pawned. Their painted mouths form shapes you cannot translate. They are reciting epics, and the syllables are not words but forms of music and origami. Then the obligatory cathedral bells turn the night pewter and silver like artifacts.

Morning was a sequence of tamed waves like a legion of miniature aqua bells, turquoise castanets. The bay suggested bolts of silk you might choose for an opera gown. Clouds lift and the harbor turns vivid and bold like Bohemian crystal, glassy cobalt and charged garnet. This is why we buy vases and flowers. This is why we compose.

Sunset was a smear of Mercurochrome, a hundred-year-old antiseptic that stings. The beach surrenders to its indigenous inhabitants, returning with their smuggled and stolen contraband arranged in haphazard bazaars, children limping in ochre rags, refuge worn as adornments. Such items may be pronounced fashion statements by the adventurous from adjacent districts that sort through remnants, often wearing plastic gloves. Who knows what *Vogue* will decree? Perhaps it's a season for red kelp shawls and bits of tin strung by hand into bands for the waist or neck? It might be the singular accessory to highlight your spring or fall wardrobe update.

There was the usual bartering of flesh and rumors, of course. Then jugglers and fortune-tellers, men who eat fire, choreograph knives, hold in their hands potents in plastic bags and tinfoil squares. Men with tarot cards, dice, and cell phones. Heroin? Boys? Girls? Virgins? Machine guns? No problem. And further, women deposited by ambiguous circumstances, abandoned at the sharp pilings of piers. Perhaps they didn't find the right soda fountain or the one to make the phone call that alters the planet's axis.

The edifices we call wonders of the ancient world, the Mayan temples, Taj Mahal, and Sphinx were only reclaimed from jungles and deserts in the past two centuries. Ruins are always relative. Perhaps the night beach here, which will disappear before dawn, deserves a Polaroid. Maybe it should be sealed in a time capsule. Let time decide its value and significance.

There were 10,000 fires of driftwood on sand, separate encampments forming rivers of flame. And new viruses in the faces of the night dwellers, in their sea-creature eyes, languid, stained, inflamed, and milky. They have sickness in their veins, their skin is ruined ink and what obsolete poisons must have looked like.

I stood on my hotel balcony, thinking the Space Age is already stale. Below, on moist sand, it was a long night of alchemy and atrocities. Somewhere, the ships came and went. It is a mythical harbor. And they still come here, leap from boats and light planes into the night waters. They are hungrier than what swims or floats near them. It's been that way in this port for a century.

The Collective Voice of Los Angeles Speaks: Marilyn Monroe

You've become the enduring collective symbol of Los Angeles. You are the city, distilled and incarnated in flesh. You are icon, oracle and prophet. How does that make you feel?

I've never thought of it that way.

What do you think of Los Angeles?

Los Angeles has a rancid gleam like spoiled lemons. It coats everything in a sort of bad childhood waxy-veneer flashback. It smells of ash in August when oranges are like eyes bulging in alleys above singed hibiscus. You're hungry. You want to eat them but they stick in your mouth and make you thirsty. Sun laminates you like photographs stuck between cellophane. People keep cemeteries in scrapbooks, little prisons they show to strangers. The images are indistinct and greasy. They could be anyone. You could buy them in a thrift store for a quarter and pretend they're your relatives. Los Angeles reminds me of children in foster homes at nightfall, when they take their clothes off. Things with ropes and pieces of metal are done to them in added-on garages with the freeway rushing in the background like a cheap sound track. It's in sync, but it has no meaning.

Is there more to this yellow? Did it inspire you to become a platinum blond?

It's not platinum, which suggests constellations and redemption. It's another yellow entirely. Asthma yellow. It comes from rotting petals and camera flashes that permanently scar your face. It leaks from clusters of stucco that remind me of blisters and lumps you get on your lips from kissing the wrong people. These are the new trailer parks with Sheetrock. Inside, people pretend to live. Los Angeles is the last spasm with an ocean view.

Has your childhood affected your choices both on and off the screen?

Everyone knows about the uncles who fondled my breasts. They kissed my seven-year-old nipples, and they got hard like marbles. A pulse like tiny moons rose from my chest. Then I knew I was a bad girl. I would always be a bad girl. It was like a private carnival just for me. There were balloons and streamers and birthday cakes with my new name in neon pink letters. And no one could tell me no.

*It's been said that you are an example of the new phe-
nomenon of personal history fusing with the sanctity
of fame, gathering a critical mass and actually trans-
forming public act. Are we really "seeing" you through
biography?*

I have no idea what you're talking about.

What's your secret?

The divinity of accident. You take a bus to Hollywood
and become a star. Anyone can do this. You don't
have to be born a countess or go to Stanford. There's
a truth beyond, more fundamental. It's all a stained-
yellow lie. How to stay thin, get pills for insomnia
and nerves. How to buy remedies at truck stops and
under bridges. You learn illicit dialects and how to
gesture with your fingers. The cinema teaches you.
Then you get money. Your alias becomes permanent. You forget your hometown and it forgets you.
Women in trailers and bungalows who change their
names to cities and jewels know. Ask Brittany and
Chelsea, Jasmine and Jade.

What do they know?

Perfume is the oil of this and all other worlds. It's
always the hour of the concubine. It's an afternoon
of incineration. I rake my sins in like poker chips, silver dollars. My defects are monumental. I am bigger

than buildings. I wear colors there are no names for, like whiskey, corn bread, amaranth, and the interior of flame. The women leaning on balconies wearing slips and names they weren't born with know. They listen to the radio, glance at weeds. It's the edge of autumn and they're not safe. Down the block, the river is falling. Stones know too much. Promises break like old branches, all the marrow leaking out. The air is fluid. I call my lies tributaries. I think myself an ocean. Swim to me. I can decipher the center of blue. I've memorized the elements. It's just a script in blue chalk. Quiet harbor, a woman drinking from a porcelain cup. She is thinking of avalanches and amputation. That's what women do beside lagoons and swimming pools.

Tell me about your shoes.

They clack on pavement, stilettos, yes, like a confusion of asphalt and thunder. They're shoes to kneel in. In this town, you open your mouth and prayer goes down your throat and you don't gag. You learn to vomit and smile simultaneously. And to wear the skin of animals, mink and fox. I can make my eyes the color of tragedy, a worn-quarry slate blue, enormous as a winter ocean. Or opening your enamel, it-was-a-gift compact and seeing no reflection. The keys don't fit. The mail gets sent back. No answer. I begin to suspect I'm dead.

How old are you?

Jesus, it's still that soiled amber out there. An afternoon for corset fittings and frayed antique cloths. It's always Thursday, pawn shops, a piece of ruined lace like nicotine on a stagehand's teeth. There is no absolution, only sequences of ravaged brass lying across lawns, concrete and oleander. My skin is a canvas like lampshades sewed from infants. I am not becoming enraged and vague. I did not ask if it was raining. Are you crazy? I am older than you. I was born older than you.

What do you dream?

Last night, I knew the dreams of a serial killer. He sees Mother carrying a wicker basket of sea green towels and just-picked apples, skin translucent as an infant. He rubs the apples Mother carries, suddenly aroused. He knows what this means. It's an image to remember with a knife. He'll tattoo this to a six-year-old. Babette. Danielle. The sisters with yellow braids on the other side of the wire fence. I am not speaking of myself, no.

They say you are often late on the set. Is this true?

They give me a script like they're doing me a favor. I'm the broad in the piece. I'm not satisfied. I want answers. I want to know why they invented rituals, calendars, and machine guns. But the scripts are always the same. Mouth to ochre mouth. Call me dog and I bark. Wrap me in rags and tell me I'm beautiful. I'd like to tell them a few things. There is cinnamon in the well. Small cities float at the edge. It's a day to bathe in almond, in a pond beneath magenta maple leaves and cathedral bells. Then they say I'm late. Everyone is waiting, staring at me, angry. I'm astonished. I don't even know these people.

Has love proved to be a disappointment?

Love is a form of contagion. The concubine knows, rinsing ginger from her hair on stalled afternoons elongated like a woman in a coma. You can get trapped in amber. It's important to be backlit and electric. I eat lightbulbs that sting. It's an interior tattoo, a road map to where I really live, strangling in static salt-breeze with too much wind and not enough skirt. You meet someone. And it's not a night or a season. It's a felony.

What are your regrets?

I have remorse, sure. I didn't save enough summer, when my arms were tanned like adobe, clay pots, and leather saddlebags. I stood by Santa Monica Bay, my lips like burned camellias, water a drained anemic blue like a legions of stillborn waves near my feet. I didn't have my stilettos. Maybe I lost them. Sunset was smeared iodine and I wondered what I did wrong. It was a paralyzed dusk heavy with loss, smelling like a two-day-old bruise. The world was a harbor where my ship never sailed. I wanted a benediction. I held my breath. I waited for revelation, some indication, however remote. I wished on stars. I was deliberate and graceful. I whispered. I didn't break a single glass. I was careful with my shadows and the shapes my hands made. I forgot to be brazen. Nothing. Just palms in wind, ragged and exhausted. The same mute pause. And someone lied when they said I was wearing just panties and no bra.

What would you like to do?

I imagine having a child. If the studio let me. It would be summer. My daughter would wear a dress of cotton printed with wisteria and peonies. There would be no radio, no television. I would be wild with wine, draped in a kimono long to my ankles. I'd stand on Spanish tile, pretending to be a dancer. My daughter would see me in a homemade wooden swing, how my shoe fell off and I was laughing, eating pears, saying it wasn't dinnertime, but tulip time, pink-flamingo and wind-chime time. I would be a mother who eats feathers and flowers. That's what's at the end of time. That and a sunset like a flock of burgundy jungle birds above a balcony where a naked woman memorizes her lines in a rented room with a broken fan.

What do you think about the form-versus-content dialogue?

When you are damaged and hungry, when you cannot separate yourself from the landscape, or know where concrete sun-gutted alleys end and your illusionary flesh begins, distinctions collapse. Day is the texture of aluminum. You open your mouth and breathe in tin and your lips bleed. When you know your name is an act of fraud, your body sculpted by truck-driver speed you blow the costume designer's boyfriend for, it is the end of words. Form? Content? Is that a game they play at dinner parties? There is a vast conspiracy of hierarchy and privilege. I've observed this. Entire vocabularies, tables of elements, formulas. But this has nothing to do with me. I know I'm unprepared. Each moment has complexities you need a calculator for. Let them go to the moon. Build a Bloomingdale's on Pluto. The radio will still burn my ears. I'll still have to show my breasts, sad moons, so tired. It's an inexorable fact, like the weather, men who drink too much and punch you. And the rent that gets raised, cars that break, sons who disappear, while you stand at a window in a rusty dusk half convinced you're about to jump. There is no content. I am pure form, incarnate. Is that the answer you want?

Would you consider living a different life?

I imagine myself with leopard-skin pants at a party where the couples are married to each other. They hold drinks with miniature pink parasols in them. Men talk about stocks, and women mention colleges for their children. I could have a new name, classy, like Emily or Anne, with an "e." I'd go to tea wearing a gray skirt and cameo broach, like a minister's wife. Seasons would stop coming like a fever or rash. Wind would sound like cellos and I'd dye my hair to mimic oiled auburn autumn wood. I would have a daughter who practiced piano and kissing in hallways painted aubergine, which is French for eggplant. You think I'm stupid? I would listen to my daughter playing Chopin and consider the elegance of a sudden death, like an air crash, the hydrogen bomb or an injection of morphine.

Are you concerned by the rumor that the studio may not renew your contract?

Listen. Arson is a form of love. It's a shaping tool like a kitchen knife or a fountain pen you sign autographs with. The forest like the heart is outlined in neon and flame. It's not an organ but a peninsula with harbors and history and bells. Then night comes, with ambulances and moans from a multitude of cumulative betrayals. Being fired from the job and divorced is the least of it.

Can you give me your version of what happened yes-terday? For the record?

I stood on the set and could not move. I was like a prop, a costume, a breakaway bottle. I couldn't deter-mine what the room was supposed to be. Walls were the texture of hypnosis. It wasn't somnambulism but something strange and abrasive, like walking in your sleep and drowning. My throat hurt. I refused to speak when they gave me my cue. My mouth was numb and scratched. I felt glassy, intoxicated by the fragrances of the set lights, the deliberate architecture of glare. I thought about miniature insects trapped in amber. That's what movies are. I felt the sticky glue of it on my legs. If I moved, I'd fall down. Stalling is also a direction, a way to drown standing up. Outside was an afternoon of burning women. I was going to name my daughter with words that sounded like bells and winter water. The name was growing in my mouth, fists of plum in my throat. I closed my eyes. Then the man from the magazine asked me, *Do you trade in pretenses? Is deceit another tool, like lipstick and a compass? Do you think you're an icon? Does that provide a justification? Do you believe mythology is forgiveness?*

I looked at him and began screaming.

Hunting and Trapping
Aunt Sarah

*S*O IT'S YOU. I WAS EXPECTING FEDEX. Sure, you all show up, sooner or later. You have babies and bring them. You come in Chanel. You come in shamatas, shawls and veils, metal hoops and hooks in your faces. You look like you're from a sect. You go to the Wailing Wall and Rome. Tibet and Prague. Then here. I'm like the last stop.

Which one you are? You all change names, dye your hair green, purple. Shave your heads. All of you bizarre. Schlepping around that *Bhagavad Gita.* Hinduism. Zoroastrianism. Now the Kabala thing with the red strings like bracelets cutting off circulation.

I'll tell you something. You look like you're trying to crawl back into steerage.

I can't see good. Are you Ruthie's daughter, with the tattooed girlfriend and motorcycle? Mike and Faye's, the architect who joined a convent? Wait. You're the one who ran away, disappeared, right?

They come for information, like I'm the identified repository, a clandestine library. The old aunt and last one standing. Maybe I have scrolls in the drawers, maps, charts. They say they're gathering ethnographic data. Irving's kid, a boy so disturbed the government pays him to just stay home on the sofa, wanted to make a film, no less. A documentary. So many questions and I tell them the same thing. No solved equations at this house. No crystal ball. No mystical resolutions. I don't know anything.

Stop trying to get back to the Dark Ages. You think they knew something then? 900. 1900. They add zeros on calendars. Batteries instead of torches. Nothing changes. It's still the Dark Ages. They just adjust the numbers.

My father came on a passport he took from a dead man. He was vague. Surnames were automatically Anglicized. Borders changed in wars. I was told to forget. It's been thirty, forty years. But I remember you. Didn't you bang your head against your typewriter at school? Last time I visited, you had bandages on your face, gauze, adhesive. Looked like you'd been in a car crash. You kept attacking your sewing machine and typewriter. "I must reject obvious reactionary patriarchal forms of oppression." You were so dramatic and sincere it was pathetic, frankly.

I visited maybe half a dozen times. We lived in the Valley. Getting over the hill was an expedition. It was a different world then, like black-and-white movies, staying married, trolleys, hats with veils, and gloves in every color. Who rode airplanes? Movie stars and presidents. Half a century of grainy footage running too fast or slow, patches of decades slide by, charcoal, indistinguishable.

You want specifics? I'm an archive? What do I know?

Your mother was a surprisingly good cook. It's astonishing because they barely had twigs and flint where her ancestors came from, much less stoves. And this was Los Angeles. Eating is an obscenity there. Anything is better than weight gain. Alcoholism. Pedophilia. Drug addiction. Kill a wife here or there. Bulimia. Shoplifting. Eighteen months in Lompoc for an understandable tax evasion. Fraud. Gambling-induced bankruptcy. These things can happen to any-one. But size 8 is an uncontestable crime, like wearing a sign that says PATHOLOGY on it.

Eating in L.A. consists of a bottle of imported water and acts of mime. A little performance-art piece where you move food from one end of your plate to the other, without making oral contact with your fork. Your mother watched her weight. We call that anorexic now. In this respect, she gave the physical impression of being normal.

It's curious, but your mother possessed an entire compendium of complicated recipes. Tender brisket with carrots and potatoes. Chicken stews with livers. Lamb shanks with tomatoes and gravy. These aren't meals you just throw together. They require rituals of initiation and supervised instruction.

Don't tell me. You wanted this obviously enhancing

knowledge, but there were too many rules. I know. You had to sign a secrecy agreement to get into your mother's kitchen. It was like dealing with classified documents. The scrub-up regulations were terrifying. It wasn't a kitchen. It was an operating room. A depository of centuries of bacteria. You needed hygiene protocols to insure no germs contaminated the foods, implements, or surfaces. You didn't just go into her kitchen. It was like NASA Control Center. Special garments, soaps, antibacterial agents.

Fear of desecrating the food, the horror of making mistakes was paralyzing. We're already genetically and environmentally dysfunctional on a biochemical level. It's taken generations of unnatural selection to produce the symptoms we have. There's so much anguish in our neurological system, we're uncoordinated, physically off balance, and awkward. I mix up left and right. I tried ballroom dancing. Hopeless. There's something wrong with my peripheral vision and depth perception. My body can't separate anxiety out of oxygen molecules. I take a breath and agitation accumulates in my nerves like nests of pathogens. It forms the Jewish plaque that leads to insanity.

Making a mistake is a Jewish sin. Break something, it's going to cost. A repairman will be have to be summoned, beseeched, vetted, negotiated with, placated, and after a protracted period of shared mourning, ultimately paid. By the time your mother had you scrub with scalding water, shampoo your hair twice, and put on a hairnet, you were dazed, in a panic you'd commit an error resulting in a Cossack or Nazi repairman entering your apartment. You trembled and fell into a fugue state, incapable of memorizing instructions. And your mother didn't have recipes. They were like spells, incantations, whispered ingredients and amounts. Nothing written down. Just inaudible syllables escaping from the side of her mouth through the mesh of your sterilized hairnet.

So you didn't progress past your despair of spilling? That's normal. To spill in your mother's kitchen was like having a radiation leak. A meltdown. Three Mile Island and Chernobyl, simultaneously. Stains on the antibacterial-treated surfaces was a problem so monumental, it compared to Hiroshima. You and your decedents were permanently damaged. Blood would leak out your eyes and ears. Your children would be born without limbs and their faces lack symmetry. From that spill on, you carry webbed feet and withered limbs in your womb. In fact, spilling endangered the whole human race.

Your mother had emergency precautions for spilling. It had to be mopped up immediately, before it dripped on the floor and into the water supply, where hundreds of thousands would give birth to genetically defective offspring. And it would be your fault, of course. The perpetrator. Word would get out. They'd come and hunt you down.

Your mother was always showing off her rolls of paper towels. They proved she wasn't white trash or a wetback like your neighbors. She had kitchen paper but no one was allowed to use it. Her version of a decorator accessory. Paper products were treated like heirlooms in those days. They were supposed to be passed on as part of the dowry. But using a paper towel in a non-life-threatening situation was a flagrant indulgence. There were moral implications. It was an indication you were headed toward Jewish hell.

In the event of a spill, there were specified procedures. Use your own flesh to absorb the excess. Throw yourself down. Roll your body in it. Eat it. Use your mouth and tongue. If that first line of protection failed, there was the sponge. A sponge could be employed in extreme cases, with adequate disinfection and bleaching afterwards. This was superior to paper towels, which once used, had to be discarded.

Every time a paper towel was used and thrown away, your parents looked like they were on the train to Auschwitz. It was like throwing an infant off the cattle car, hoping some peasant would pick up the free kid and use it for labor. You know, not stomp or sauté it, but think, hey, Mary, this could grow into a farm slave. Let's keep it around. Chain it up next to the goat in the barn. See if it can survive on manure and straw. Your mother had the same roll of paper towels in precisely the same place on the kitchen counter as an aggressively visual statement of prosperity. It was there, enticing and unused, each time I visited.

Your mother had a compulsion for cleanliness beyond the approved standards of that period. Plastic in layers on the sofas, presumably so they would last at least two or three lifetimes. Coasters for glasses tactically placed every three inches on all stainable surfaces. But your mother went beyond an environment that would pass CDC Level 4 Containment, like they have for Ebola outbreaks. Your apartment appeared as if no one had ever been in it. A museum for the living where indisputably costly objects are blatantly displayed but never touched. They were strategically located too high or low, or set behind clever barricades of wire baskets filled with artificial fruits and flowers that make tactile contact impossible.

Our ancestors crawled out of shacks, hovels, crevices in mountains, and seaboard tenements. Apartments with a candle only lit when the boys did math homework. They thought a chicken wing and a cabbage leaf was a gala. Where did they get this obsessional neurosis about cleanliness? Maybe they thought it was American. It was their concept of assimilation through extreme hygiene.

There were strictly enforced refrigerator regulations. Never leave the refrigerator door open. Room-temperature air could infiltrate, inciting negative bacterial reactions from insufficient cooling. It had to work harder to maintain its optimum temperature.

The thermometer was disturbed. The bulb might need to be reactivated. Fluctuations were calculated and reflected on the monthly bill. It wasn't a refrigerator but an elaborate ecosystem. It was a minefield.

Your mother only let the refrigerator open for three seconds. You memorized what was inside, its precise location, grabbed and ran. Or you lost your chance. No open-door ruminations. Or that even more profound blunder, gratuitously moving foods with bacteria-laden hands. To this day, when a refrigerator door shuts, I think of amputation.

I still have certain phobias about garbage disposals. We possessed one, it came with our standard-issue apartment. But we weren't permitted to use it without precautions. My family wasn't so different from yours, believe me. The garbage disposal was our equivalent of the Barrier Reef. It could only be touched at pre-approved intervals. Accumulated debris was sorted and measured. Then cold water was run, and it had to be cold, for a timed-by-clock five minutes. After the timer clanged, the extremely gradual introduction of the material ensued. We stepped back when we turned it on because it might erupt or explode like a volcano or hand grenade. Who knew what was inside? Blindness was an inevitability. A constant cost-benefit analysis was required. Was it worth such a risk?

Our typical procedure was to turn it on and run from the kitchen. Then we switched it off, letting cold water run for another timed five minutes. It wasn't an appliance. It was like entering a combat arena. And never put your fingers in, even when it's shut off. It could chew up your hands. They thought it was an entity with volition and an emotional range, purposes, strategies, conspiracies.

You need to remember the times. Fifty years ago. People didn't know how electricity worked and didn't want to know. Who could comprehend what bizarre whims and cruelties controlled wires and circuits? Only Gentiles understood this. Or those other Jews, who played clarinets, went to college and became doctors, neurosurgeons, and psychiatrists. Jews instinctively know there's a problem with the brain. They want to talk about it, examine, analyze, get scalpels and dig the crap out. But it was obvious to us that you needed advanced degrees to deal with garbage disposals. Math classes, anatomy lessons, metallurgy, blueprints. It was better to consider the garbage disposal as another decor item.

Using the garbage disposal invited the possibility of breakage. We were afraid of the provocative serrated-metal crevice. We'd been instructed to never put our hands inside, but once I caught a spoon in there. It was like the sound of one thousand trains arriving at the platform in Dachau on a December night in a blizzard. A repairman would have to be called. My family gathered around, drawn by the sound of gravel, cattle cars, and primitive thunder.

They stared at me like I'd just ratted them out to the Gestapo.

Repairmen were the worst-case scenario, up there with bankruptcy, police arrest, deportation, and heart attacks. Engagement with the hostile alien population was required. The yellow pages were studied; attempts to determine which service was the least life threatening were analyzed. Telephone calls were made to relatives we ordinarily ignored. Consultations. More vetting and negotiations.

Repairmen were abhorred hillbillies and anti-Semites. They hated Jews, who killed Christ, the Pope told them this is 1215 and it made an impression, believe me. Also Jews owned all the banks and stole infants for demonic sacrifices. Repairmen were thieves with union cards. They kept them in their wallets next to their swastikas.

Los Angeles was an open wound waiting to be stitched. Actually, L.A. was where your parents went when every bookie from Hialeah to Saratoga was after them. It was the ticket for the trip they never thought they'd have to take.

I remember you, though. Walking in circles with an umbrella and poetry book, your head bandaged. Your hands, too. Didn't you break your sewing machine? Didn't you punch it, throw it on the floor and kick it? You broke your foot and wrist?

These days, your parents would be identified, labeled and legally medicated. You'd have a hotline number to call. They'd be in compulsory court-mandated counseling. They'd have handicapped parking stickers. Your mother would have a low jack on.

So, you wore secondhand clothes from Jewish services? That's how the world was. You've traveled? Has it changed? Poor girls routinely shunted to vocational classes. That's axiomatic. Sure, no one considered us capable of more than serving as wives, waitresses, and secretaries. Maybe a schoolteacher or nurse. If we got lucky.

Your parents were so proud of Los Angeles. They took me on a tour. Massive building sites, holes like craters, orange cranes on Wilshire Boulevard like a swarm of Mesozoic predatory birds. They were constructing freeways and shopping malls with eight layers of underground parking and lobbies with atriums and fountains. Your parents thought they were being built for them.

But the city being born was a kingdom of starlets in bikinis with backyard tennis courts and swimming pools, gardeners, chauffeurs. We were incidental to the process. We were refugees from an internal undeclared war that no one wanted.

I'll tell you what we are. We're slippage. Hawthorne's dark forest, forget it. There are other more insidious lethal landscapes. So, you wouldn't have the vocabulary or technical skill to explain this for decades? So you failed English and Home Economics? You were swathed in gauze last time I saw you.

OK, for you it was worse. Your parents had washed up in the hallucinatory assemblage on sand without seasons. They're utterly unprepared in a remote half-built village at the edge of the incomprehensible Pacific, which is definitely larger than the Volga or Danube.

They didn't understand the sea breeze loitering above streets with cartoon names like Marine and Seaview, Hibiscus and Dolphin Drive. Who could take that seriously? It's a circus, your mother used to say. Lamplight cast an oily sheen on the lawns. Bougainvillea, which they couldn't pronounce, grew colossal through fences, and night was dense with alien fragrance. The constant rhythm of the ocean, the complicated choreography of oleander and bird of paradise were elements in a kind of jazz they couldn't comprehend.

It was like the ocean poured through the mesh screen doors and windows. Tides and currents, an abundance of desert sand in hot winds they assumed was a deliberate irritation. An insult, a warning in code. Chinese and Thai spices, Mexican salsas, and boulevards they couldn't pronounce. La Brea, San Joaquin, La Cienega, Calle Lago, Vista del Mar. They were unanchored. They were not in New York, where streets had numbers and rules. But where were they?

They couldn't conceive of accommodation and networking. That takes a generation. Your parents got sucker punched and went down for the count. The neighbors with their drawls, beer, allergy to books, and anti-Semitism repelled them. They dismissed them as repugnant, ignorant farmers. Somewhere along the oxcart, steerage, and Greyhound route, your parents developed a profound distrust and aversion for peasants. Anything from the ground disgusted them. Dirt was proof of a defective IQ. They were acculturated by omission. They couldn't identify or memorize the local vegetation. So they removed them from their perception.

They had an antipathy to tropical fruits. You had blue jay-pitted peach trees next to your bungalow. These were forbidden. Only farmers knew how to deal with such things. And they were apparently free. Nothing free could be good. They were probably laden with illegal insecticides that caused deafness and palsy. Or they were part of a clandestine scheme involving fines and loss of citizenship.

Once I brought a few mangoes. Mangoes were vehemently outlawed. They were illicit, Mexican or worse, the pinks and oranges of obscene pagan rituals. There were implications they couldn't decipher. This confused and frightened them. Mangoes had nothing to do with them. It was like politics or horseback riding, country clubs, joining a synagogue or the PTA.

I visited maybe a dozen times. Your parents withdrew further into their exile in the new gulag. They acted like they were undercover. They subscribed to the *New Yorker*. They had internal monologues with Pauline Kael. Let the Santa Ana winds blow. Let phosphorescent algae from Santa Monica Bay stink like corrupted saltwater, sanguineous from ruptures and curses.

I agree, it's paradoxical. They had a capacity for detail, but couldn't adjust their basic framework. They couldn't synthesize. They were conflicted and defeated. The erratic bursts of coherence they couldn't sustain. They read reviews of Broadway plays they'd never see. They'd been drifters and now they were banished. OK, it was frustrating. I sympathize. They were isolated, bankrupt, antisocial, and suffering from some form of sudden onset and protracted tropical-shock syndrome.

Actually, they were like the last colonists in the compound after the regiment pulled out and the empire collapsed. The only recognizable communication that remained came by subscription. Then they regressed into bitter mute submission. They cultivated a cynical indifference.

Let the neighbors beat up their kids and wives in whatever language the slaps and kicks were issued in. The boys would end up in juvenile detention on their way to prison. The girls they called no-good would disappear when their bastards started showing. Your parents decided to just read through the apocalypse, smoking cigarettes and drinking scotch. Let the sky set in radiation orange and magenta streaks and seizures. They kept the blinds shut, reading on the plastic-wrapped sofa with one lamp on.

Lights were strictly rationed in your family. You needed a sanctioned reason to be in contact with them. Homework was optional, right? Your parents had come a long way. They knew who Marx, Freud, and Einstein were, but their knowledge was superficial and impressionistic. School wasn't legitimate. It was like the house, and they knew it couldn't be beat. The world was a casino with electronic surveillance, and all the tables were rigged.

Grades and test scores were for another species. Maybe Jews who went to Torah class, played golf and violins. It didn't apply to us. There was just the diminutive partial illumination from the one lamp per occupied room allotted. Electricity was an extravagance. Los Angeles was a medieval oasis. Coalitions of warlords at the utility companies had incomprehensible capabilities and powers. And they had special rates for lost Jews with a trail of betting debts behind them.

Then they got a car. This was significant. They had to go to driving school and pass tests. Like all aptitude measurements, it was geared for Gentiles who intrinsically knew the rules, possessed by birthright the capacity for calculations like feet and yards. That came from centuries of owning property you got to keep. Some drunken Cossack didn't ride in, kick your ribs until they broke like twigs, and say it was his farm, he had documents and proof. So they had performance anxiety when demonstrating their vehicle knowledge and skills. It took them the maximum four times to ultimately get licenses. Each trip to the DMV was like a Gestapo interrogation.

It was a secondhand car, of course, green and embroidered with rust. Cars presented a vista of new possibilities, all with virulent, malignant complications. They didn't know anything about machinery. In New York, you had a problem, you called the super. But here? And a private car, with its unfathomable engine and incomprehensible vocabulary consisting of inimical words like valves, gaskets, alternators, plugs. Who was prepared for this?

Your car was a junker. It clanked, sputtered, and emitted black smoke from the tailpipes. The brakes were unreliable. It lacked acceleration. Hills were a peril. Your parents found the city impossible to navigate, with boulevards they couldn't pronounce and no identifiable clues rising from the flat relentless vegetation. So they memorized three east-west boulevards, Pico, Santa Monica, and Olympic. In between, they had a system with patterns, like turn left two streets after the corner with the giant neon doughnut sign.

Their routes were designed to avoid hills and cul-de-sacs where they might be stranded for hours or days at the mercy of passing anti-Semites. They had handmade maps for getting to the supermarket, the bakery, and doctor. Only three boulevards were authorized. Once an essential dispensary was identified, no deviation was permitted. The safe havens were known, and no matter what happened, how the service and quality deteriorated, how the manager got cancer, went blind or deaf, and the front door came off its hinges, it didn't matter. They went back forever.

There were stringent regulations about the car. It could only be used for emergencies. And you had to go directly to and from your destination. This was called "no circling." If you intended to go to the bakery and there wasn't a parking space immediately available, you drove on. You did not turn and go around the block. That would be the transgression of "circling." They only managed rudimentary parking skills, like the white painted lines in parking lots or vertical parking meters. Fitting the car in, manipulating it between other vehicles, was not in their repertoire. If you arrived at your destination and parking wasn't waiting, it was an omen. You knew it wasn't meant to be. No bread that day or that week. Back to the apartment.

The worst thing about the car was the breakdowns. The ritual of contact with a car mechanic. In their pantheon of repairmen viewed with foreboding and loathing, car mechanics were the top rung. They were farmers with sharp implements in pouches attached to their bodies. And tools on shelves and in metal boxes. It wasn't a garage. It was an armory. After the redneck thieves took off their tar-encrusted uniforms, they put Klan sheets on. They were all cousins and had the same names, too. Jeb. Red. Wade. Gus. Tex. Wes.

A car mechanic was their version of brain surgery. The discussion first, the exploration of contingencies, the methods of how to survive the ordeal. You had a gas station on the corner. Your father approached with two bottles of bourbon, one in each hand, raised up high like twin flags of surrender. The offering to Billy Joe or Russ. The propitiation, visible from half a block. Then the agony of lifting the hood and the inspection of the metal anatomy by flashlight. Your father stood in the garish sun sweating, attempting to appear to comprehend, through the local drawl, the various valve and hose malfunctions. The car wasn't having an inspection. It was a pre-autopsy biopsy.

Don't even mention phones. Toll calls still haunt me. There was an era before cell phones and national minute plans. The age of area codes. Calls within your own zone were free. Each outer region had a progressive cost. Tolls were the bells from hell.

The theory was simple. It was better to die than make a toll call. If one deviated to the point that necessitated a toll call, wasn't it preferable to just lie down on the pavement and let vultures come? If you miscalculated your gas supply or strayed from your appointed three-boulevard path, wasn't death the honorable option? A toll call was a variation of not keeping up with the oxcart. Find a gully with a bush and call it a scenic retreat. Pound your head against the rock. Maybe you'll strike oil. Then you can call us from your own phone. You left the compound. Disneyland? Vegas? It's not our responsibility. Then they were emotionally excised.

We weren't hillbillies or wetbacks with a grandmother who had a phone and shared it. The matriarch who took messages, told bill collectors, landlords, parole officers, and assorted government functionaries they had no idea who you were or where you went. We didn't have a designated mediator with the outside to keep information flowing. Who was in the hospital. Who died, had a baby or anniversary. We didn't want to know.

We had our own phone. It came already installed with the apartment. But just looking at it cost money. It was a treacherous instrument. All communications were suspect; sentences were rife with nuances, complexities, and entreaties. Grief and disaster came through wires, hazards and tragedies. It was better not to know. When the phone rang, we ignored it. The sound was like howls wild animals made, ambulance sirens, and women and children being slammed against walls in Spanish or Korean. We kept the black metal device under pillows.

Long-distance calls were unthinkable. Once

somebody ventured beyond the state, they ceased to exist. They crossed more than a geographic line. There were indisputable monetary consequences. Whatever lay beyond San Bernardino was unimaginable. It was like the Kalahari or Gobi. Deserts of cactus, deformed trees with spikes like arthritic fingers. Dehydration. Cannibalism. Leaving the state was to assume the risks of a wagon train and what happened at Donner Pass. Anyone requiring long distance was summarily deleted.

Collect calls were like reciting the rosary or differential equations. It wasn't in the family frame of reference. We had passwords instead. We figured out that the telephone apparatus could be subverted. There were loopholes. It was possible to receive a collect call. We just couldn't accept it. This was how they created and employed codes.

Let's say we received a collect call from Shelly. This was encrypted. Shelly actually meant the person in question had gotten where they were supposed to, the occasional funeral or wedding, and they anticipated surviving. If the collect call was from Marvin, it meant the person in question had a problem, a complication. They needed assistance. That was unfortunate. One tried to absorb as much information as possible in the voice, deconstructing nuances of tenor and pitch. It was verbal tea leaves. Then the deciphering by triangulation within our free zone. Calling others in our area code, gathering, transmitting, and formulating options, counteroffers and fallbacks. It was the Jewish equivalent of palm reading.

I don't remember much after high school. I was already waitressing at a deli. A split shift, but still a start. Then I got married and moved. We lost touch with your parents. Some argument with your mother. Something about a chicken, who owed who a buck. You know those people. A wrong look, a facial expression they don't like, and you're excised.

I never went back. But I still retain a certain irrational response to telephones. Direct verbal communication is too intimate for me. It's worse than leaving the refrigerator open or letting a fork lodge in the garbage disposal. A ringing phone connects you to anyone, anything. Cataclysm. Ambush. Betrayal. Answering a phone is like voluntarily letting an armed stranger in.

I have an answering service and a phone-message machine. I don't check my service under any circumstances and erase all messages immediately without listening to them. If it's important, the communication will get through. I rate caller ID as one of the great inventions of the century. I put it up there with the birth control pill, hormone replacement, Internet shopping, and chemotherapy. I rarely answer a phone. If the text says unknown, I consider it an omen. It isn't meant to be.

So you just came here and found me? One by one, you all come, tremulous with expectation. It's sickening and redundant. You want to find villages in Russia, third cousins in Bulgaria or Budapest? Enough already. I tell them the Inquisition is over. Stop interrogating yourself.

Don't even start with me. You're the one who ran away, the flower child, with the poetry books, the umbrella, your face covered in bandages? Didn't they fine for you for breaking those typewriters? You went to Berkeley, right? Then you disappeared.

I don't know anything else. You want more, hire a private detective. Seeing you brings back nightmares. Remember, you don't have my address. And don't ever come back.

P.S.
House for Sale

A SPECTACULAR PROPERTY HAS JUST come on the market and I suspect it will appeal to you. It's an 1849 meticulously renovated farmhouse. The walls are original planks from barn wood, all floors are red maple or white oak, and 100-year-old railroad ties are used as ceiling beams throughout. Windows present panoramic views combined with complete privacy. The unique setting and dense foliage render curtains unnecessary.

This mini-estate has four bedrooms, four bathrooms, formal dining room, sunroom, and library, stone fireplaces, and a woodstove in an upstairs room the seller describes as her "study." The property includes a 40-ft. swimming pool with Amish handmade gazebo, orchards, 7-ft. high deer-proof fenced gardens, flagstone paths, and natural ponds.

Located in a college community, this property offers four seasons and nearly ninety acres in a rural village in the magnificent Allegheny Mountains. An apple orchard, still productive, and hundreds of miles of maple forest surround it. In autumn, forests are sequences of reds and yellows turning intoxicating shades of burgundy, wines and clarets. Autumn will particularly appeal to drug addicts and alcoholics. You get drunk just looking at it.

You've seen the photograph on the back of the *New Yorker* that says *experience fall* and in tiny letters indicates the picture depicts Pennsylvania or Vermont? This mini-estate looks just like that.

This unique house is perfect for the artist, the aesthetically inclined, and other intellectually self-contained individuals. Talk about finally finding the place to read the Russian novels and history tomes you've been carrying around for decades, placing in one bookshelf or another, waiting for the serenity such serious and weighty endeavors require. It's also the spot to write that novel or memoir you've been secretly gestating.

This property includes a separate (unfinished) cottage that cries out to be converted into an artist's studio. Simply throw your kiln in and let the clay fly. Or stick your teenager there. It's got electricity. Just give your kid a down sleeping bag and come back in spring. You'll both be happier.

Of course, the outbuilding could be inexpensively completed and serve as guest quarters for your numerous friends from the city who will be visiting you "in the country." Or it could be your recreation room. Put in a pool table, a jukebox, and popcorn machine and practice your ballroom dancing. Or just keep a cot in there. You can use this cottage during virulent marital communication failures. Alternatively, you could rent it to a college student in exchange for household help and yard work. You could even turn it into a bed and breakfast. Talk about the ultimate multipurpose room with unlimited possibilities!

This separate cottage building is also built of hemlock and is part of the original 1849 dwelling. Like the "Big House" it has charming features. It's equipped with two wall-to-floor windows facing a grove of pine trees and the swimming pool. This is the shop you've always wanted. It's time for furniture carpentry right now. Alternatively, it could be your gardening and winter storage area, or officially sanctioned meditation and yoga room.

The potential for this outbuilding is limited only by your imagination. You could install your sick older parents there. Assisted living is a gray area. Consider the options this cottage presents. You could tie up a family member during a bipolar episode that's gone over the borderline. Let them scream their throats raw. No neighbors in eye- or earshot. You can detox your wife from one of her infrequent but unfortunate recurring heroin binges in the safety of your own home without expensive rehab situations and the nasty paper trail that results in raised insurance premiums. In fact, this cottage is excellent for people with dysfunctions they don't want publicly recognized or privately analyzed.

The house was entirely renovated, for substantially

more than the original cost of the property, by a family from Los Angles who thought they'd reached the end of their journey and would be living there until death. They installed skylights on the porches in the front of the house, which is generously planted with wisteria, clematis, and lilac bushes. The porch surrounds the house, amplifying the 360-degree unimpeded view.

Each garden bed is lined with stones pried from creeks and individually hauled here by the woman seller, Mrs. X. She was an artist from Los Angeles who engaged in abnormal acts of bravado gardening because she thought it a triumph over her personal circumstances. People apparently raised her with eccentric edicts about not interacting with earth. She came from a disturbed urban family who irrationally feared the ground. Soil was stigmatized. It was for "farmers." Learning to grow tomatoes, carrots, corn, squash, herbs, and flowers was an achievement for Mrs. X. It was a method by which she temporarily transcended her circumstances. Or that's what she thought. It seemed plausible. But then again, this woman has a flexible notion of what comprises normalcy.

This house, this mini-estate, could be a miracle for a family trapped in a city who realize they must radically change their life or die. Simplify and redefine yourselves while simultaneously providing an absolutely secure environment for your children, with continuity and stability. No locked doors or drive-by shootings in our town. Your children can wander forest paths observing wildlife and birds in a setting that would ordinarily require a significant admission fee.

You won't have that life-endangering three hours on a good day commute anymore. Our college and town are one traffic light away and it's all downhill if you choose that 2.2-mi. scenic walk. You and your spouse won't both have to simultaneously work and engage in ruthlessly oppressive child-related activities such as driving through combat zones for orthodontist appointments, soccer practice, dance and music lessons. You don't need to schedule your children's playdates months in advance and endure the agonizing anxiety of knowing these events are auditions that have nothing to do with play.

It's more informal in our community. Your children don't need to speak three foreign languages, play the cello, and be practicing Sanskrit translations in their spare time. They don't need to have their first haiku chapbook published by their thirteenth birthday. If your kid has four limbs and can remember which school bus to get on, you won't have a problem.

Almost everything you need is right here in our college town with its one red, amber, and green traffic light, or in our neighboring "big" town, a mere twelve miles of indelibly rustic forest road away. In addition, your children will be transported by a traditional yellow bus to a public school where they'll have the classic American egalitarian rite of passage so many in urban configurations are deprived of, namely attending an educational institution with youths from diverse socioeconomic backgrounds. Your children will attend classes with the offspring of professors, including those of our college president, town mayor, and one doctor. Your children will also have daily interactions with our town folk and those from the hills beyond our one traffic light. Their parents are farmers, small-business proprietors, and, candidly, an overwhelmingly significant number of them are unemployed.

This just-listed mini-estate implores you to retire early, right now, while you have this unique opportunity. With the increasingly unfathomable complexities and uncertainties of the global corporate economic fabric, where an envelope of anthrax in Portugal or Peoria can wipe out your entire portfolio, this is where you can retire, today, with your current savings. Do it while you're still healthy, only have hypertension and moderate cirrhosis, say, and get that chance for the new American dream, the rural second life.

This is the house, shop, or artist space you've craved but thought unobtainable. Imagine your solitary country walks, probing the meaning of existence and the etiology of your own pathology. You are naturalist, philosopher, and psychoanalyst as you stroll majestic maple-forest dirt roads and paths. Plumb your psyche at leisure, charting your synapses like a cartographer landing on a new planet. Carry a notebook, tape recorder, sketchbook, and camera with you.

Asking price for house, multipurpose cottage, fenced gardens, flower beds lined with stones from creeks throughout the county, ponds, and adjacent acres: $165,999. This is the ultimate Topanga Canyon or Marin County multimillion dollar house (not counting the additional acres, which would be unavailable and unaffordable in those locations) for a fraction of the price.

Does this sound too good to be true? That depends entirely on you, your values, daring, and level of desperation. Of course, there's something of a downside. But that can be said of all cities and towns, in all regions, in any area of the world.

If you've had enough sun that shatters in your face like a special-effects radiation sequence, and years measured in malicious incisions of inextinguishable summer with air quality you need a Geiger counter for, then you may be ready for the four seasons of our region. For a variety of geographic reasons, our sun is often screened completely for weeks or months. It's a filtration our seller, Mrs. X., called Attica gray, in honor of the prison a mere seventy-five miles to the north, and in recognition that oppression comes in a surprising spectrum. If you are interested in gray, sun-erased gray, storm and cloud gray, grays like tin, pewter, charcoal, thunder, aluminum, ash, and gravel, you'll be guaranteed a spectacular hands-on experience here. And remember, you'll have your encounter with gray from 360-degree views while watching deer from your windows, mere feet from where you stand, eating your apples or tulips, depending on the season.

Our seasons are not strictly textbook. Spring and fall vary, adding to the challenge of home maintenance, emergency roof, window, and plumbing repair, and gardening. They also provide a visual excitement and drama not even imagined in Los Angeles. Some springs come on cue in April, subtle hyacinths and crocuses pushing up through snow, just as the gardening manuals indicate. After the winter coma that smells of ice and gray wind that is beyond antibacterial, is, in fact, a total absence of anything identifiably biological, the first points of what will be peonies and iris are a sort of miracle. At such junctures, Wordsworth and odes to daffodils are not merely obsolete footnotes but three-dimensional vivid yellow realities that are mind altering.

Sometimes there is no spring because winter can linger here. It can just drop anchor and hang over the valley like a gray battleship you wish you could use a few cruise missiles on. Just shoot it down and don't even bother with salvage. In truth, winter lasts at least seven months. If it's a year with an indeterminate autumn, Indian summer may or may not occur. Some autumns, you can walk with a tank top through the forest that makes you drunk until November, memorizing the palette of maples with a rare intimacy. You instinctively possess a new vocabulary. Apricot, plum, aubergine, russet, ochre. Reds are divided into flame, burn, fire engine, vermillion, crimson, banner, and blood. Yellows are distilled into distinct categories. Amber, honey, straw, the fleshy, refined Asian gold of amulets, bronzes, blond and platinum.

If you're from Los Angeles, you've probably never understood the symbols of harvest time. You can't comprehend mutilating pumpkins until you've grown and gouged your own. Or the Halloween significance of bats. But after you've lit the candle in your carved pumpkin, it provides an unexpectedly fine light to observe flying creatures circling your porch, aiming for your door.

In other falls, our first ice storm strips the trees overnight and early October looks like Hiroshima after the blast. Stark limbs begging for a mass burial. Snow may arrive in October and remain on the ground until June. You will need to alter your wardrobe. Our seller, Mrs. X., sprained both of her ankles before divesting herself of certain favored footwear and recognizing that fashion statements are an encumbering complication here. For very special occasions during Christmas, high heels are carried in a plastic bag and mud boots replaced by more precarious footwear once you've successfully navigated and entered the residence or public hall where you're going. No matter how winds howl and snow accumulates, the below-freezing temperatures, exacerbated by wind chill, are not a problem in the house in question, which is for sale, because the entire mini-estate has been upgraded with forced-air heating in every room.

As to summer, which looks precisely like the *New Yorker* photographs of New England, there are variations. For instance, the family selling this house, Dr. and Mrs. X., arrived in an August of brutal heat in an incendiary intensity they thought feral and appealing. In truth, summer tends to be cool and unpredictable. The general rule of thumb is this. When you hear that hundreds are dying from heat-related incidents in *both* Chicago and Philadelphia, that means it's probably warm enough here to use the swimming pool. Since the sellers heated the 40-ft. flagstone-lined pool, you may count on additional days of swimming opportunities. Barbequing by the poolside and swimming under moonlight are indescribably pleasurable during such summers.

Our stars are extraordinary. Recently, while sailing through French Polynesia, the sellers of this property were disappointed during their Constellation Lecture to find the sky above the unpolluted South Pacific to be vastly inferior to their normal night skies. Or what would be normal if gray installations of clouds weren't stationed above their residence, if an armada of metal warships hadn't moored above the house and sealed the sky shut.

This is a climate ideal for individuals who have a capacity or inclination for winter sports. Skiing is available a mere forty-five minutes of country road beyond town. Dr. and Mrs. X. are not skiers, not even cross country, and failed to participate effectively in acquiring snowshoe activities, didn't hunt, and refused to leave their house during ordinary weather-related events such as blizzards and black-ice storms, which Mrs. X. labeled virulent conditions.

Potential buyers should also have a tolerance for insects. Mosquitoes, horse flies, and gnats bit the sellers. They wantonly scratched and subsequently infected themselves. Despite a coating of insect repellent applied directly to the skin and long-sleeved shirts and pants sprayed with another layer of insecticide, Mrs. X. was plagued by insects. The local remedy is high doses of vitamin B. Despite coming from California, Mrs. X. is not of the New Age persuasion and claims to be an unrepentant pagan. She refused this espoused proactive supplement and remained the only person in town to carry insect-repellent spray in her purse. It can be substantiated that she was, on numerous occasions, the only person bitten or stung during outdoor occasions. It can also be verified that she was often swarmed.

As to our town itself, it's like all human configurations, a backdrop for your own personality. It's what you, the buyer, interpret it to be. After a grotesque adolescence, and deliriously difficult adulthood enmeshed in the peculiar complexities of Los Angeles, our sellers were at first satisfied with our community. Mrs. X. enrolled in art classes at the college, despite her inability to draw, creating monoprint hieroglyphics with chopsticks and twigs. Dr. X. taught advanced graduate courses and conducted research of a classified nature.

Frankly, we have no idea what he was doing in his laboratory. There's speculation Dr. X. was a notorious underground 1960s antiwar activist, an infamous bomb maker who always carried a concealed Beretta and used university facilities to manufacture illegal substances. It's been whispered that he robbed armories and sold weapons to the Black Panthers and Weathermen. There's absolutely no evidence for this. A sign on his office door reads, *When they give it to you, it's called medicine. When you give it to yourself, it's called a drug. Is that politically correct?* No one knows what that means. Since the lettering resembles the chopstick-and-twig hieroglyphic alphabets Mrs. X. was compulsively producing, we believe she taped the sign there. In any event, we don't care.

Despite being a Los Angeles woman, Mrs. X. learned how to cook in this skylight-adorned maple and oak kitchen, and invited other senior faculty to

their house for weekly dinners. They availed themselves of our small-town college offerings, lectures,
musical productions, and increasingly occasional
films and diminishing literary events.

Mrs. X. joined the town playhouse, where she
"acted" for the first time, and wrote and directed several plays. Our audience consists of fifteen to twenty
individuals who attend our theater group as they do
church, with regularity and uncritical acceptance.
Such a venue apparently did not prove sustaining for
what Mrs. X. termed her hereditary narcissistic personality disorder.

Our seller volunteered at the local hospital, where
her duties included transporting patients from their
beds to medical imaging and back. She also as-
sembled enema kits. Mrs. X. imagined herself an
ethnologist and engaged patients in personal con-
versations. Since it is a tiny rural hospital, dialogue is
limited. Patients are often extremely old and come to
the hospital to die. Or they're members of the fifth-
generation underclass never discussed by anyone
associated with the college. The illegitimate daughters who are now the mothers of their own illegitimate children and grandchildren. They've been on
welfare for generations. They haven't worked since
the railroads and dairy farms. Consigned to typically
unheated trailers, such people, usually women, have
no medical insurance. Their standard procedure is
to wait until they're sick enough, have pneumonia

on top of their emphysema, and can then be legally admitted by ambulance as emergency patients. Or they arrive by ambulance after being beaten by boyfriends. Broken bones and skin requiring stitching allows them hospital access.

Being in our hospital is perceived as a vacation. No one punches them or calls them stupid fat sluts. They receive laundered sheets and pillowcases. Food on a tray arrives at regular intervals and second portions are frequently available. In fact, the hospital is the only reprieve the less fortunate members of our outer community have, particularly during winter.

Our seller came to know certain patients' stories and what it is to be a female generations into welfare, and how imprisoning isolated rural villages are for the uneducated. Low self-esteem is epidemic. Travel is rare; few had been to New York City or professed an aspiration to do so. Satellite television, alcohol, and abusive transitory alliances with males provide the contours of their trailer-park typographies.

During her volunteer work, budgets diminished. Rules for welfare were upgraded, making it impossible for such women to meet the requirements, which included three job interviews per week, even though they had no vehicles, public transport is nonexistent, and there aren't three available jobs in their category in the entire county. As a consequence, they were monetarily punished. Mrs. X. said that even possessing a car, a resume of extraordinary workforce performance, and several advanced degrees, she doubted she could satisfy the welfare system.

Eventually, Mrs. X. found the hospital less fulfilling. Being mildly dyslexic, she failed to adequately integrate the procedures for placing patients on a gurney while simultaneously correctly loading the oxygen tanks of the many with emphysema. Still, kneeling before the obese, emaciated, or rarely touched, placing socks on their weathered and callused feet, she had a sense of something she described as almost spiritual grace. After her third bacterial infection from direct contact with patients, Dr. X. concluded she lacked the awareness and immunities for her position.

Recently, on her farewell tour of the area, the seller admitted to a sense of frustration with our neighboring "big" town. The few independent clothing and gift shops have gone out of business. The town is stripped bare. Main Street is five bars, the police station, spires of churches, a few dozen home-medical-supply stores, fire station, pool hall, convenience stop, and fast-food dispensary. Our motto is this. We don't have any progress and we don't want any. Of course, that has nothing to do with you, the prospective buyer.

It took years for our sellers to realize that one can't simply inflict a college in a region of entrenched Appalachian impoverishment and expect to be insulated from its effects. After all, it comes on the school bus with your children. The inhabitants of trailers and derelict shacks and barns, which is all that's left of their farms, often have no electricity or telephones now. This socioeconomic devastation infiltrates our town, faculty, and its vision. Our college is also collapsing back on itself, declining in enrollment, endowment, and leadership. There are rumors the college is going to officially close and the buildings converted into a prison. The untenured have been fired. Program review is in progress. No one knows what criteria will be employed, by whom, or when.

After decades in an increasingly underfunded academic failure, a feudal coalition of mediocrity was encouraged and sustained. This is not a place for big ideas. After all, we're a county without a single psychiatrist. Think in terms of pencils and erasers. Or don't think at all. Use the same syllabus for twenty-five years. Just don't rock the boat. The waters here are perilous, floods and droughts, the necessity of incessant emergency home and road repairs, the inadequacy of an infrastructure. Now our professors can taste sea in their mouth. It's too salty to speak. If they had an idea and attempted to verbalize it, they might drown.

Our non-unionized faculty is terrified of unemployment by methods that might be generously termed random and arbitrary. The ship is going down. Even Deans are frantically searching for flotation devices. They're still standing in line, not overtly shoving or knocking the aged or frail to the ground. Not yet. They still go to church and plant their bulbs on time. But the fear produces a further level of something feral and rancid littering the gray air. Mrs. X. has called it clawlike and an improvement.

Of course, the sellers emphasize that the medieval politics of a disintegrating institution have no impact on you. While it illuminated the sellers' vision, this has nothing to do with the prospective buyer, who will have little involvement with the college, other than occasional discretionary events. And you, the buyer, can still enjoy lunch at the town's coffee shop, knowing the proportion of PhDs and MFAs at the adjoining Formica tables, eating reliable comfort food offerings such as grilled cheese sandwiches and pancakes, are statistically astronomical compared with other cities. Such a ratio would not exist in Los Angeles.

A small town, like a major modern center, is a tabula rasa. Our particular seller might never have bothered to garden. No one forced her. She might have pursued her book of *Birds of the Northeast* and walked with her imported binoculars, recognizing the profusion of species as they migrated north and south, often stopping to build nests in the mini-estate's orchards. Mrs. X. might have acquired skills to recognize more than robins and finches, but she found birds difficult to classify. Everything seemed big and black to her. Where is the line between big and medium-sized, black and charcoal? And, of course, the insurmountable identifying question, *how are they flying?* They're doing it well, with authority. *How are they flying?* They're using their wings, damn it, Mrs. X. screamed with rage.

Our town offers a multitude of avenues for self-expression. There are no rules, though church affiliation and excessive alcohol consumption are recommended. But you are free to manifest your second-life rural personality as you choose, employing inexpensive empirical trial-and-error methods. The sellers have a friend who trout fishes and acquaintances who ride bicycles on our breathtakingly scenic country roads. Or hike. Mosquitoes do not bite them. Some have telescopes or chart constellations by eye alone; here where stars are a text in icy chips, and the Milky Way is a current in the sky, a silvery tributary you could track for years.

It should be noted that our town even offers opportunities for political engagement. Mrs. X. joined the local Rural Democratic Club, which consisted of eight overtly involved individuals. We vote Republican, even when Roosevelt ran. In this capacity, Mrs. X. worked for the election of Hillary Clinton. The highest extent of their goal at its most fervid, I've been told, was to produce a double-digit loss. The overall state tally was at issue. A 10 percent vote would have been a triumph. Our seller met Mrs. Clinton several times. When the First Lady accepted an invitation to speak at the college, Mrs. X. had an hour of one-on-one with her. As she repeatedly noted, and I mean repeatedly, in L.A. you'd have to be Barbra Streisand to get that.

The problems encountered by our sellers have nothing to do with what *you* create of this multi-million-dollar property that you can buy for a mere $165,999, which is negotiable. The fact that our seller couldn't master driving in snow or ice and pronounced our closest city, Ithaca, with Cornell University a mere eighty miles east to be an impossibility, is a perverse and eccentric response. Just eighty miles of largely paved road away, Mrs. X. could have availed herself of mental health professionals, natural food stores, yoga supplies, and medical specialists. Clearly, no one is that driving challenged.

But if you are, the emergency room in our neighboring "big" town is a timed-by-clock eight-minute drive. And unlike Cedars Sinai in L.A. or similar renowned facilities in urban centers, you are immediately admitted. Our emergency room sees few bullet or knife stabbings and rarely receives patients in handcuffs. Whatever your symptoms are, you won't be ignored for days in a waiting-room plastic chair with CNN blasting. Our nurses won't chastise you for taking up space when beaten children are being carried in naked from police cars and you aren't even bleeding and don't have a temperature of 105.

As for the winters, our sellers claim they were consciousness raising. Winters required that they depart our community completely for extended periods, frequently months. In their former pre-relocation mode, our sellers rarely left Los Angeles.

It was like inhabiting the entire planet already. However, faced with Allegheny winters, Dr. and Mrs. X. traveled extensively through China, Southeast Asia, Europe, Mexico, the Caribbean, India, Nepal, Egypt, and Africa. They told me our town was excellent preparation for the Third World. They were already accustomed to rudimentary communications, transportation, medical care, and that *can't-do* attitude prevalent in less developed nations.

If you purchase this magnificent property and your children need braces, the seller must inform you there is one orthodontist in our "big" town, and all the economically fortunate children receiving this procedure have identical teeth arrangements. In a recent tragic alcohol-induced car crash that claimed the lives of four of our teenagers (precisely thirteen seconds after they started to drive), there were complications. Since the kids were incinerated, they had to be identified by their dental records. Due to the nature of orthodontia here, the standard scientific procedures were protracted.

You probably want to know why the sellers have put such a staggeringly gorgeous property on the market. Why are they leaving, after eight years of gardening and faculty gatherings, after nights constellations outlined themselves with the specificity of neon graffiti while they swam, it's rumored, naked in their pool, watching deer graze by moonlight?

As I mentioned, our sellers are from Los Angeles.

During their years of transition from the accumulated atrocities of Southern California, they came to understand, by seasons, by increments of wind howl and fox mew, that the event-horizon landscapes they had internalized are permanent. One can heal a bit, recuperate while throwing some clay pots and pulling weeds from perennials, but they will still bury you with the scars.

Mrs. X. informed me that she remains committed to stylistic experiments. Art is the audacity to render deformity as well as perfection. She is convinced art is the deliberate rejection of the known for an alchemy of risky dissections performed in altitudes that require oxygen masks. She called it engaging the mutating subtext in mortal combat.

Mrs. X. says Los Angeles is a colossus of hibiscus and sunsets in spasms resembling curry, cancer, and advanced jaundice. The archetypal abusive lash of sun-battering tenements tainted with nicotine and not enough light originate from the same faulty bulb, in West Los Angeles or the Allegheny Mountains. It's a greasy light of insults in rooms smelling of beer and unwashed shirts that become ingrained like DNA. Geography does not alter this deformed double helix.

In a stucco bungalow in Santa Monica or a trailer in Allegheny, such light numbs and becomes a starch-laminating moment, trapping one as amber does a fossil. There are penetrations of intent and violations of the spirit one knows not from criminal law but from what we dare recognize as literature. Mrs. X. believes literature is the Ellis Island of our nation's soul. It is the word alone that grants the disenfranchised legitimacy.

Naturally, I have no idea what she's talking about. I'm just selling the house. The mini-estate and most expensive property in the county, by the way. I'm taking room measurements, and Mrs. X. is babbling rapturous about sacred callings. Sometimes the burden of bearing witness is unendurable. We identify birds and constellations instead. But these are temporary solutions. Mrs. X. explained that since she's from Los Angeles, she is accustomed to tentative inexplicable resolutions that disappear without warning. Days are improvisational reinventions as you cross toxic waters.

The sellers have had their metaphorical casts, bandages, and stitches removed. They've found the core of solitude and its conjunction with landscape, internal and external. While the themes and hierarchies of civilization remain, there are centers where originality and daring are welcome. Once Athens, Constantinople, or Paris. There are trade routes for ideas, too. If such is your impulse or affliction, a one-light town in a valley between Pittsburgh and Toronto may not be the permanent residence for you.

The sellers are moving back to California. It's rumored they're going to San Francisco, a seaport conducive to radical provisional excursions and a tolerance for the aggressively and flagrantly non-conforming. They want to spend their lives as if they were a series of clinical trials. If you can translate that, let me know.

Of course, they've always been the designated town family of suspicion. Coming from Los Angeles they brought a distinctly vulgar and abnormal sensibility with them, an implication of ostentatious proclivities and affections. They probably had intimate contact with the 1960s, the sexual revolution, social activism, drugs, and God knows what. They didn't go to church. They didn't drink. Were they really our kind?

I believe the sellers were of a kind with our community. But we didn't sustain them. There is something vagrant and gypsy within their fabric, a yearning for what we might call tawdry, flagrant, and artificial, if we dared to speak, which we don't. In our town, saying certain words out loud is not acceptable. Or talking about politics, religion, governments, culture, sex, alcohol, infidelity, finances, or divorce. Mrs. X. told me that the prevalence of stringently maintained political correctness destroyed sophisticated verbal choreography. They believe our community fears uttering a politically incorrect syllable, which would be like breaking one of the Ten Commandants, and the speaker would have engaged in a deliberate sin.

The sellers prefer garish extravagance in the service of precarious and accidental revelation rather than the regulated conformity currently in national vogue. Dr. X. called it painting-by-the-numbers for the morally bankrupt. The sellers would rather have incandescent neon-infested boulevards with ersatz glittering invitations to consume than the pinched lips of neighbors who just encountered a verbal architecture they suspect isn't orthodox. Their mouths assume the shape of one who has bitten into a sour lemon. One wishes to spit it out, but recognizes that wouldn't be socially appropriate.

Los Angeles, with its media industries and barely comprehensible just-emerging technologies, slithering out from rocks like infant reptiles, the sellers symbolically miss you. They appreciate your willingness to recognize truth as permeable, to barter with each passing cargo ship, knowing the trade routes always shift. Dr. and Mrs. X. explained you don't leave Los Angeles. Rather, it's a series of insidious encounters you chance to survive. And after resting from the trauma, you strap your pack on and keep going. You are offspring of coalescing temporary junctures, millennial refugees, beyond obsolete borders.

The sellers have hit the road. They just loaded their car with the UC BERKELEY and HILLARY CLINTON FOR SENATE stickers on the bumper and drove off. Even with their tourist disguises of sunglasses and baseball caps, we don't think they'll actually get across our Homeland Security checkpoints and vigilant state and county patrols.

We suspect they're mutational bards or a subspecies we don't have a category for. There's increasing speculation they deliberately posed as upright citizens of our town so their daughter would have a normal period of stability to mature and individuate. Anyway, their kid is in law school in Boston now. They'll probably need a lawyer since Dr. and Mrs. X. are certainly anarchists. We know because they told us. Mrs. X. said she was a guerilla fighter, at war with the patrician demarcations between genres, which she called postmodern relics and vestiges of privilege that should be torched. Maybe they're arsonists, too.

But they've left a fantastic house with four completely renovated bathrooms, including one with an exceptionally well-refurbished original claw-foot tub behind. Why they needed four bathrooms, I can't say. Did I mention the apple orchard and ponds? The 40-ft. stone-lined heated pool?

All I know is that they've gone back to California. They didn't leave a forwarding address. It's as if they simply vanished. One day they disappeared. But the $165,999 is simply an approximation and absolutely negotiable. And you can call me collect.

The Graywolf Press Nonfiction Prize

Frantic Transmissions to and from Los Angeles: An Accidental Memoir by Kate Braverman is the first winner of the Graywolf Press Nonfiction Prize. Beginning in 2005, Graywolf awards this prize annually to a previously unpublished, full-length work of outstanding literary nonfiction by a writer who is not yet established in the genre.

The Graywolf Press Nonfiction Prize seeks to acknowledge—and honor—the great traditions of literary nonfiction, extending from Robert Burton and Thomas Browne in the seventeenth century through Daniel Defoe and Lytton Strachey and on to James Baldwin, Joan Didion, and Jamaica Kincaid in our own time. Whether grounded in observation, autobiography, or research, much of the most beautiful, daring, and original writing over the past few decades can be categorized as nonfiction. Graywolf is excited to increase its commitment to this evolving and dynamic genre.

The prize is judged by Robert Polito, author of *Savage Art: A Biography of Jim Thompson, Doubles,* and *A Reader's Guide to James Merrill's The Changing Light at Sandover,* and Director of the Graduate Writing Program at the New School in New York City.

Kate Braverman has been chronicling her life in poetry, short stories, essays, and novels for thirty years. Raised on welfare in the stucco slums of Los Angeles, she studied comparative literature and anthropology and graduated from Berkeley in 1971. She was a founding member of the Venice Poetry Workshop and Women's Building. Her novel, *Lithium for Medea,* is currently in its fifth edition and her work has been translated into Italian, Turkish, Japanese, and French. She is married to Dr. Alan Goldstein, a research scientist in nanobiotechnology and a futurist, and they live in San Francisco.

The text of *Frantic Transmissions to and from Los Angeles* has been set in Warnock Pro, a typeface designed by Robert Slimbach for Adobe Systems in 2000. Book design by Wendy Holdman. Composition by Prism Publishing Center. Manufactured by Sheridan Books on acid-free paper.